MANTILLA

Mantilla

The Veil of the Bride of Christ

ANNA ELISSA, OP

Foreword by
His Excellency Antonio Guido Filipazzi

OS JUSTI
PRESS

Os Justi Press
P.O. Box 21814
Lincoln, NE 68542
www.osjustipress.com

Send inquiries to
info@osjustipress.com

ISBN 978-1-965303-13-9 (paperback)
ISBN 978-1-965303-14-6 (hardcover)
ISBN 978-1-965303-15-3 (ebook)

Book design by Michael Schrauzer
Cover photograph by Allison Girone
(@LatinMassPhotographer)

This book is dedicated
to everyone who loves, upholds, and
fights for Church teachings and traditions,
not for their own sake,
but for the glory of God
and the salvation of souls.

Please pray for me.

CONTENTS

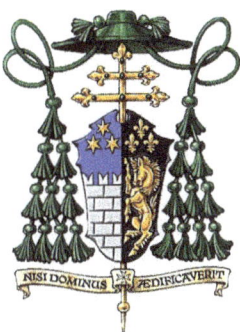

His Excellency Antonio Guido Filipazzi

TAKING THIS BOOK IN HIS HANDS, probably somebody will be a bit skeptical and will ask: why this subject, why this book? That was my reaction too.

I invite you to read this book, because it will be for many, as it was for me, a beautiful surprise. Here the author, a young woman who studies psychiatry but is well prepared also in the theological field, shares with us her experience. But the experience that she shares is not just her feelings or emotions or her personal likings; she gives us the *reasons* for her choice, that is, the reasons for wearing a mantilla during the liturgy. And therefore we find in this book historical, theological, liturgical, and practical reasons for rediscovering this practice, which was once very common in the Catholic Church everywhere.

The important thing that the author stresses in the book is that, of course, it is not enough to wear the mantilla in order to be a good Christian. The mantilla is only one of the elements of the Christian life, of the spiritual commitment in following Jesus.

What I wish for those who will read the book is to have the same good surprise that I had reading it. I hope this book will contribute to a better Christian life for many people, especially for many women, and to a deeper understanding and practice of our faith.

Jakarta
December 6, 2015[†]

[†] At the time of the book's first publication, His Excellency was Apostolic Nuncio to Indonesia.

PREFACE TO NEW EDITION

THIS BOOK WAS FINISHED ON THE Solemnity of the Immaculate Conception, in the year 2015. Little did I know that I would be writing a new preface on the exact same day, nine years later.

It is heartening to see that veiling in Mass is no longer a strange sight (I speak in regard to the Novus Ordo Mass, for at the Traditional Latin Mass it has always been familiar). Yes, it is still not as common as many of us would wish, but all great things and noble aspirations take time to grow.

Can something as simple as a chapel veil, or the mantilla, be considered "great" or "noble"? Certainly not in itself. Like all worthy devotions, it must lead us to sanctity. In other words, veiling must jump-start or accompany a woman's repentance—lifelong, faithful, *joyful* repentance—and her growth of virtues.

In areas where veiling is not yet widely embraced, the women who do veil can stick out like a sore thumb. Consequently they will likely be held to a higher standard. In areas where veiling is more regular, a different danger arises: it can become just another liturgical routine, a piece of sacred beauty we take for granted. We need to be careful so that neither of these situations may become an occasion of sin, but rather an opportunity to preach, to glorify God through the suffering of attracting unwanted attention (or of enduring monotony), and as a "whip"—as my countrymen would say—to pray better and live better.

Whether you are the only one who veils or one amongst many, reviving the practice of veiling in

Mass requires also the rediscovery of the ancient wisdom of the Church. Let our well-nourished intellect fuel our will to love. For this purpose, I hope this book is pertinent, and I pray that it will remain so for years to come.

Our faith teaches that love is the final measure. Does the practice of veiling — and our other devotions — propel us to greater love of God and neighbors? Does it introduce us to a purer life free from sins? Does it help "conform us to Christ Crucified," as St. Catherine of Siena would exhort us to do?

Finally, the words of Saint Maximillian Kolbe are worth some reflection: "When you kneel before an altar, do it in such a way that others may be able to recognize that you know *before Whom* you kneel."

Therefore, let us veil in such a way that others may be able to recognize that we know, and love, the One for Whom we veil.

Anna Elissa, OP
Bogor, December 8, 2024
Solemnity of the Immaculate Conception

A LITTLE MORE THAN ONE YEAR HAS passed since I wrote my online testimonial about the chapel veil.[1] At the time of its publication, I had been veiling at Mass for three years. This means that up until the completion of this book, I have been regularly veiling for four years.

During those four years, many positive changes have occurred with respect to the chapel veil, especially its specific lace variant, the "mantilla." Initially, the mantilla was foreign to the eyes of Indonesian Catholics. At that time, in all the churches I went to, I often found that I was the only woman who veiled. Naturally, I felt alone and out of place.

The funny thing is, the first round of support came from a few of my Muslim friends. They once saw me wearing the mantilla, so they asked, "Why do you veil? Is that a Catholic tradition?" I said yes, and after some explanation, they extended their support, citing modesty as their primary reason.

Now the situation has changed for the better. The mantilla is cropping up everywhere like mushrooms in the rainy season. In Indonesia, the word "mantilla" has become a catch-all term for chapel veils in general. In some churches now, I am graced with the company of other veiled women. Most of them, like me, wear the actual lace mantilla. Some others

---

[1] My testimonial may be accessed here (in the Indonesian language): https://luxveritatis7.wordpress.com/2014/05/15/mengapa-saya-mengenakan-kerudung-misa/.

wear a scarf or a pashmina. Those new friends of mine come from a variety of backgrounds and ages, but the majority belong to the OMK (*Orang Muda Katolik*; Catholic youth) group.[2]

Traditions revived by the youth? Indeed it is not impossible! The Traditional Latin Mass, the Novus Ordo Mass celebrated in Latin, and the appearance of Gregorian scholas in parishes—many of the Church's traditions are being rediscovered, reintroduced, encouraged, and/or enlivened by young people. It is uplifting to see that more and more young Catholics discover this "pearl of great price."

The return of the tradition of veiling at Mass has been featured in HIDUP Magazine No. 35, Year 69, August 30, 2015. The front cover was titled *Kaum Kerudung Masuk Gereja* ("The Veil Clan Hits the Church"), a title that was worded somewhat derogatorily, although the actual articles shone a positive light. This proves that the practice of veiling at Mass is spreading and is starting to catch the attention of both the sheep and the shepherds alike. Unfortunately, there is not yet any complete and definitive catechesis on the devotion. I am personally in agreement with Fr. Sridanto Aribowo, head of the Liturgical Commission of the Archdiocese of Jakarta; in an interview with HIDUP, he pointed out that "people who wear the mantilla must be able to responsibly account for their faith." This echoes the words of our first Pope: "Always be ready to give an explanation to anyone who asks you for a reason for your hope" (1 Pt 3:15).

---

[2] "OMK" is a demographic term referring to Catholics aged 13 to 35 years and unmarried. It is also an organisational term referring to the parochial ministry that specifically caters to this population.

I feel that I share the responsibility of providing good catechesis and witness on the chapel veil. This catechesis is primarily intended for women who have been veiling regularly and those who are still considering adopting the practice, so that they may know and love this tradition even more. However, it is my hope that Catholics in general, both men and women, both senior and younger generations, both the laity as well as the religious and the clergy, may benefit from this humble book.

I pray that the chapel veil will be better received and introduced more broadly as a way for women to be more intimate with their true Beloved, Jesus Christ in the Blessed Sacrament. I also pray that this tradition will not be only a seasonal trend, a way of "jumping on the bandwagon." I want this humble little mantilla to really be a physical sign of women's internal response to the universal call to holiness.

Finally, together with St. Teresa of Avila, let me assert: "If I should say anything that is not in conformity with what is held by the Holy Roman Catholic Church, it will be through ignorance and not through malice. This may be taken as certain, and also that, through God's goodness, I am, and shall always be, as I always have been, subject to her. May He be forever blessed and glorified. Amen" (*Interior Castle*).

Anna Elissa, OP
Bogor, December 8, 2015
Solemnity of the Immaculate Conception

TERMINOLOGY

THERE ARE THREE TERMS RELATED TO
the topic of this book that need to be defined so that
they do not cause confusion.

HEAD COVERING

A "head covering" is a general term to refer
to all pieces of clothing or accessories that
are used to cover the head. In the Christian
religious context, head coverings include
mantillas, scarves, shawls, pashminas, head-
bands, hats, caps, bonnets, and so on. Ladies
who want to practice covering their heads
at Mass but do not have actual mantillas
may choose one of those alternatives.

CHAPEL VEIL

As inferred from its name, a chapel veil
refers to any kind of veil worn at Mass, or
for private prayer inside a church, such as
at Adoration. So this term is more specific
than head covering but less so than mantilla.
Nowadays, "chapel veil" is often taken to
be synonymous with "mantilla."

MANTILLA

A mantilla is a characteristically Roman
Catholic veil usually made of lace or lace-
like materials. The word "mantilla" is a
diminutive form of the Spanish word
"*manta*" (English "cape"). The mantilla had
its beginning in Spain around the end of

the 16th century and was then introduced
to Latin America. The original mantillas
were a fashion item worn to important
events, both secular and religious. The term
"Catholic mantillas" arose to distinguish
between ordinary mantillas and those worn
to Catholic Mass. In recent centuries, the
mantilla has been adopted by the whole
Church as a pious practice.

In this book, the terms "chapel veil" and "mantilla"
are used interchangeably in liturgical contexts. When
discussing the more general topic of covering one's
head, the terms "head covering" and "veiling" are used.

Virgin Annunciate
Antonello da Messina (1430–1479)

CHAPTER 1

Veiling in Sacred Scripture, Apostolic Tradition, and Church History

WHEN MODern Catholics hear the word "veil," it is almost immediately associated with religious traditions such as Islam or others of eastern origin, such as the Indian culture. The fact is, the custom of Christian veiling, especially during worship, is an ancient tradition that has an apostolic root, as confirmed by St. Paul (cf. 1 Cor 11:1–16).

How, then, did the teaching and practice of veiling in the Christian context develop?

This chapter is an overview of the practice in the light of Scripture, the apostolic tradition, and the history of the Church, beginning from the Old Testament to the 1983 Code of Canon Law. As an overview, this chapter is not designed for in-depth study, but rather to show the "connecting thread" of the history of Christian veiling.

Readers who are less interested in the historical origins of veiling may skip this chapter and read the following chapters.

OLD TESTAMENT

If we examine Scripture, we will find that veiling has long been part of the tradition of God's chosen people. In the Old Testament, Israelite women veiled for the purpose of modesty and to protect their dignity. In Genesis, we read how Rebekah quickly veiled herself when she was about to meet her future husband, Isaac.

> Rebekah, too, caught sight of Isaac, and got down from her camel. She asked the servant, "Who is the man over there, walking through the fields toward us?" "That is my master," replied the servant. Then she took her veil and covered herself. (Gen 24:64–65)

Rebekah modestly veils herself with respect and reverence for Isaac, who is described as the "master." She is as yet unmarried. In the Book of Daniel, we meet a woman named Susanna, who had veiled herself in a context different from Rebekah's, for she is already married. Susanna was a beautiful and pious woman wrongfully accused of adultery. When the two evil men were prosecuting her in front of her husband and relatives, they forced Susanna to take off her veil.

> Susanna, very delicate and beautiful, was veiled; but those transgressors of the law ordered that she be exposed so as to sate themselves with her beauty. All her companions and the onlookers were weeping. (Dan 13:31–33)

From the text we see how the action of omitting a veil when feminine modesty calls for it or tearing off a woman's veil is looked upon negatively, even considered a disgrace, by Scripture.

NEW TESTAMENT

The passage of the New Testament that explicitly commands women to veil—and the text that is often cited by modern veilers—is the eleventh chapter of 1 Corinthians:

> Be imitators of me, as I am of Christ. I praise you because you remember me in everything and hold fast to the traditions, just as I handed them on to you. But I want you to know that Christ is the head of every man, and a husband the head of his wife, and God the head of Christ. Any man who prays or prophesies with his head covered brings shame upon his head. But any woman who prays or prophesies with her head unveiled brings shame upon her head, for it is one and the same thing as if she had had her head shaved. For if a woman does not have her head veiled, she may as well have her hair cut off. But if it is shameful for a woman to have her hair cut off or her head shaved, then she should wear a veil. A man, on the other hand, should not cover his head, because he is the image and glory of God, but woman is the glory of man. For man did not come from woman, but woman from man; nor was man created for woman, but woman for man; for this reason a woman should have a sign of authority on her head, because of the angels. Woman is not independent of man or man of woman in the Lord. For just as woman came from man, so man is born of woman; but all things are from God. Judge for yourselves: is it proper for a woman to pray to God with her head unveiled? Does not nature itself

teach you that if a man wears his hair long
it is a disgrace to him, whereas if a woman
has long hair it is her glory, because long
hair has been given [her] for a covering? But
if anyone is inclined to be argumentative,
we do not have such a custom, nor do the
churches of God. (1 Cor 11:1–16)

This text, together with Ephesians 5:22–24,[1]
should not be interpreted as "a text of oppression of
women." What needs to be understood is that there
exists a mystery of the order of creation that places
all creatures, both angels and men, in a hierarchy.
In his commentary on 1 Corinthians, St. Thomas
Aquinas describes this hierarchy and its origins in
Christ, saying:

It should be noted that the natural order
of things is so arranged, that lower beings
imitate higher beings, as far as it is possible.
Hence even a natural agent, being superior,
makes the thing it acts on similar to itself.
Now the primordial principle of the produc-
tion of things is the Son of God, as it says in
John (1:3): "All things were made through
him." He is, therefore, the primordial exemplar, which all creatures imitate as the true
and perfect image of God. Hence it says in
Colossians (1:15), "He is the image of the
invisible God, the firstborn of every creature,
for in him all things were created."[2]

---

[1] "Wives should be subordinate to their husbands as to the
Lord. For the husband is the head of his wife just as Christ
is head of the church, he himself the savior of the body.
As the church is subordinate to Christ, so wives should be
subordinate to their husbands in everything."

[2] *Commentary on 1 Corinthians* 11:1–3, no. 583.

Aquinas continues, making a comparison between the angels, who are the first to emulate God's divinity, followed by other creatures, and the prelates of the Church, who guide the faithful towards God. Church prelates become a model for mankind because they receive their example from Christ and are therefore required to become examples for their sheep.

> Just as angels were first to imitate the exemplar of His divinity, but secondarily the other creatures, ... so the exemplar of humanity is chiefly proposed to be imitated by the prelates of the church, as being higher. Hence the Lord says in John (13:15): "I have given you an example that as I have done, so do you." Secondly, however, the prelates informed by the example of Christ are proposed to their subjects as exemplars of living: "Being examples to the flock" (1 Pt 5:3); "To give you in our conduct an example to imitate" (2 Th 3:9).[3]

Whether the superiors be prelates or angels, from both of these passages it is clear that various creatures serve as examples to one another in this mysterious hierarchy.

The principle of the order of creation is used to explain the relationship in the divine family that is made up of God, man, and woman. Woman is subject to man and man is subject to God; this does not demean women, but this relationship is symbolic of the mystical relationship between Christ and the Church. Man is an image of Christ, because Christ became incarnate as a man. During worship, men

---

3 Ibid.

have to be bare-headed to symbolically acknowledge and preach Christ's Incarnation as a man. Meanwhile, a woman, who is an image of the Church, veils herself because she believes that Christ has become incarnate as a man to sanctify His Bride. The veil is not a sign of a woman's personal holiness; it is a sign of the Church's holiness, because She is sanctified by Christ.

Therefore man is not the party that receives the "upper hand" from woman who is subject to him. On the contrary, man carries a great responsibility towards woman, that is, to sanctify her and to make her more similar to Christ, the exemplar of all creation. This oft-forgotten responsibility is described more clearly in Ephesians 5:25-30:

> Husbands, love your wives, even as Christ loved the Church and handed himself over for her to sanctify her, cleansing her by the bath of water with the word, that he might present to himself the Church in splendor, without spot or wrinkle or any such thing, that she might be holy and without blemish. So [also] husbands should love their wives as their own bodies. He who loves his wife loves himself. For no one hates his own flesh but rather nourishes and cherishes it, even as Christ does the Church, because we are members of his body. (Eph 5:25-30)

The authority of man over woman is like the authority of Christ over the Church, and woman's subjection to man is like the Church's subjection to Christ; this relationship is not based on slavery or fearful intimidation, but rather on love and self-sacrifice. The concept of woman as the image of the

Church reaches its ideal culmination in the figure of
the Blessed Virgin Mary. In the words of Pope John
Paul II: "Mary is the model and icon of the Church."[4]
This symbolic relationship is best summarized in the
following table.

TABLE I. MAN AND WOMAN IN DIVINE ANALOGY

MAN	WOMAN
God the Father	Christ
Christ	Church
Logos	Soul
Image of God	Image of man

Veiling for women in church is a physical expression of the same concept, because the veil is a "sign
of authority" (1 Cor 11:10: "*ideo debit mulier* potes-
tatem *habere supra caput*"). A woman wears the "sign
of authority" over her head to indicate that there is
authority or power over her; this acknowledgment
requires a great deal of humility, trust, and loyalty.
The Church, represented by a woman, covers the
beauty of her head in order to give glory to God,
under Whom the Church always abides in love. Just
by covering her head, a woman may proclaim a great
truth, namely that God rules over all mankind and
all creation, and to Him we must subject ourselves.

But why did St. Paul command women to veil,
when elsewhere he said, "Long hair has been given
[her] for a covering?" The reason is similar to why
a married couple wears wedding rings, though the
Sacrament of Holy Matrimony itself is valid even
without rings. This is because humans need visible

---

[4] John Paul II, *Mulieris Dignitatem*, no. 27.

signs of invisible reality. We are physical creatures who respond more readily to physical, visible symbols. A woman's veil is an affirmation of what is already proclaimed by nature.

CHURCH FATHERS

The Church Fathers are great teachers who taught and laid the foundations of the Christian faith during its early years. The Church Fathers include those who were students under the Apostles themselves, such as St. Clement of Rome, St. Ignatius of Antioch, and St. Polycarp of Smyrna, down to the last of the Church Fathers, St. John Damascene (676-749). These Church Fathers supported veiling for women, especially during Mass. Their support came in a variety of forms, from stern admonitions to gentle advice. Their particular interpretations about why women should veil may be stronger or weaker, closer to or further from what is essential, but it is valuable to see how unanimous they were concerning the practice itself, which they saw as established by the word of God.

Among the Fathers, Tertullian (160-220) gave more stern and emphatic advice. He stressed that both virgins and married women are required to veil as a discipline. In his work *On the Veiling of Virgins*, he wrote:

> But we admonish you, too, women of the second (degree of) modesty, who have fallen into wedlock, not to outgrow so far the discipline of the veil, not even in a moment of an hour, as, because you cannot refuse it, to take some other means to nullify it. [5]

---

[5] *On the Veiling of Virgins*, ch. 17.

Tertullian was adamant in his testimony that the "apostolic Church" held the custom of veiling for married women and for virgins—that is, the veil is appropriate and edifying for all women in every state of life. He also defends the practice as a characteristically Christian one, "lest any ascribe the custom to Greek or barbarian Gentilehood."[6] It was St. Paul who visited the Corinthians and imparted the practice, and so Tertullian writes that "at this day the Corinthians do veil their virgins. What the apostles taught, their disciples approve."[7]

Another eminent author, Clement of Alexandria, wrote around the year 190:

> Woman and man are to go to church decently attired, with natural step, embracing silence, possessing unfeigned love, pure in body, pure in heart, fit to pray to God. Let the woman observe this, further. Let her be entirely covered, unless she happen to be at home. For that style of dress is grave, and protects from being gazed at. And she will never fall, who puts before her eyes modesty, and her shawl; nor will she invite another to fall into sin by uncovering her face. For this is the wish of the Word, since it is becoming for her to pray veiled.[8]

St. John Chrysostom (349–407), quoting St. Paul, connected the practice of veiling with the presence of angels:

---

6 Ibid., ch. 2.
7 Ibid., ch. 8.
8 *The Instructor*, III.11.

> The angels are present here . . . Open the
> eyes of faith and look upon this sight. For if
> the very air is filled with angels, how much
> more so the Church! . . . Hear the Apostle
> teaching this, when he bids the women to
> cover their heads with a veil because of the
> presence of the angels.[9]

St. John Chrysostom maintained that a woman who
refuses or renounces the veil does not gain the glory
of man; on the contrary, she falls from her dignity.

> But if any say, Nay, how can this be a
> shame to the woman, if she mount up to
> the glory of the man? We might make this
> answer; She does not mount up, but rather
> falls from her own proper honor. Since not
> to abide within our own limits and the
> laws ordained of God, but to go beyond,
> is not an addition but a diminution. For
> as he that desires other men's goods and
> seizes what is not his own, has not gained
> any thing more, but is diminished, hav-
> ing lost even that which he had (which
> kind of thing also happened in paradise),
> so likewise the woman acquires not the
> man's dignity, but loses even the woman's
> decency which she had.[10]

St. Ambrose of Milan (337–397) spoke indirectly
on veiling and the danger involved in neglecting
this custom. In his treatise *On Virginity*, Ambrose
condemned any kind of immodest practice, among
which is the casting off of the veil.

---

[9] *Sermon on the Feast of the Ascension.*
[10] *Homily XXVI on the First Epistle to the Corinthians.*

> Is anything so conducive to lust as with
> unseemly movements thus to expose in
> nakedness those parts of the body which
> either nature has hidden or custom has
> veiled, to sport with the looks, to turn the
> neck, to loosen the hair? Fitly was the next
> step an offense against God. For what mod-
> esty can there be?[11]

The Doctor of Grace St. Augustine (354–430), who
was converted by St. Ambrose, in his treatise *On
Holy Virginity* discussed the pride of some virgins who
deliberately transgressed the principles of Christian
modesty for their own pleasure:

> Either by more elegant dress than the neces-
> sity of so great a profession demands, or by
> a remarkable manner of binding the head,
> whether by bosses of hair swelling forth,
> or by coverings so yielding that the fine
> net-work below appears: unto these we
> must give precepts, not as yet concerning
> humility, but concerning chastity itself, or
> virgin modesty.

In the above quotation, St. Augustine offers a
new perspective on veiling. He did not admonish
women who did not veil, but rather admonished
those who did veil and yet let their hair hang loose,
or who wore a veil so thin that the hair beneath it
showed. Evidently the ancient Christians aspired to
simplicity and opacity of clothing. We can conclude
that St. Augustine realized the importance of veiling
for women, and that the veil must be worn properly
and seriously.

---

[11] *On Virginity*, III.6.27.

Here it is clear that the early Church faithfully practiced St. Paul's teaching in 1 Corinthians II, even to the level of what we would consider extreme, such as covering the entire body all the time. Women prayed veiled, while men prayed with bare heads; this practice was understood and implemented throughout the Church in Europe, the Middle East, and North Africa.

THE BLESSING OF THE VEIL IN THE RITE OF THE CONSECRATION OF VIRGINS

In the Medieval Age, usually understood to be from the fifth century to the end of the fifteenth century, veiling for women was common and admirable; this may be deduced from paintings originating from that age that portray pious women veiling themselves. Additionally, in the Medieval Age, the veil acquired a new, more religious meaning as a "crown" for consecrated virgins.

In Catholicism, there are three states of life: religious celibate, lay celibate, and married. Every one of the faithful is called to holiness, but the path we take to reach that noble destination depends on the specific calling based on our state of life, and also on our secondary vocations, such as our education and occupation. As for those women who are called to walk the path of celibate lay people, many of them devote themselves as consecrated virgins. They usually form an association or a fellowship in order to help and strengthen each other in their services to the Church. This is regulated in the Code of Canon Law, Canon 604.[12]

---

[12] Can. 604 §1: The order of virgins is also to be added to these forms of consecrated life. Through their pledge to follow

The practice of consecrated virginity can be traced all the way back to the beginning of the New Testament, to the figure of the Blessed Mother, who herself was a consecrated virgin (cf. Lk 1:34). The Church even commemorates her consecration on the Feast of the Presentation of the Blessed Virgin Mary on the 21st of November. In the first few centuries of Christianity, we see a number of female martyrs who were consecrated virgins, such as St. Cecilia, St. Agatha, St. Agnes, St. Lucy, St. Philomena, and St. Apollonia. Other great names like St. Gemma Galgani, St. Catherine of Siena, and St. Rose of Lima were also laywomen who consecrated themselves and lived as celibates.

In the Roman Rite, a specific liturgical celebration for the consecration of virgins has existed since at least the fourth century, according to St. Ambrose's writing about the consecration of his own sister, St. Marcellina. The liturgy was celebrated by Pope Liberius on Christmas day in the year 353, and was conducted in a Holy Mass.[13] One element that can be found in this liturgy is the rite of blessing and conferring a special veil upon these virgins.

Throughout history, the text of the liturgy of consecration of virgins, including the blessing of the veil, underwent development and maturation. In the tenth-century *Pontificale Romano-Germanicum*

Christ more closely, virgins are consecrated to God, mystically espoused to Christ and dedicated to the service of the Church, when the diocesan Bishop consecrates them according to the approved liturgical rite. §2: Virgins can be associated together to fulfill their pledge more faithfully, and to assist each other to serve the Church in a way that befits their state.

13 *On Virginity*, III.1.1.

(PRG),[14] we find a beautiful text for the blessing of the veil, which has been preserved in Pope Leo XIII's *Pontificale Romanum:*

> O God, Head of all the faithful and Savior of the whole body, sanctify with your right hand this covering of the veil, which your maidservant, by reason of your love and the love of your most blessed Mother, namely Mary ever Virgin, is going to put upon her head; and may your protection ever preserve undefiled in soul as well as in body that which is mystically expressed to be understood by it, that when she shall have come to the everlasting reward of the saints, she herself having also been made ready with the prudent virgins, you conducting [her], she may be worthy to enter the marriage of everlasting happiness. Who lives and reigns, God, world without end. Amen.[15]

---

[14] The *PRG* is a tenth-century collection of Latin documents concerning the Roman Rite liturgy of sacraments and sacramentals that may be celebrated only by the bishop, for example, the consecration of holy Chrism, Sacrament of Confirmation, Sacrament of Holy Orders, consecration of a church building, and consecration of virgins. *PRG* and its revisions (e.g. Pope Leo XIII's *Pontificale Romanum*) only include the specific rites themselves, not the entire Order of the Mass or the Divine Office; these have been collected separately in the *Missale Romanum* and in the *Breviarum Romanum.* Pope Leo's *Pontificale Romanum* may be accessed online at: http://laudatedominum.net/files/pontrom.pdf.

[15] Caput omnium fidelium, Deus, et totius corporis salvator, haec operimenta velaminum, quae famulae tuae propter tuum, tuaeque Genitricis beatissimae Virginis Mariae amorem suis capitibus sunt impositurae, dextera tua sanctied-fica; et hoc, quod per illa mystice datur intelligi, tua semper custodia,

From this blessing, we conclude that the veil is now infused with a noble meaning, that of purity and glory, especially heavenly glory. The veil is taken to mean renunciation of the world and its ornaments for the love and service of Christ. The shape of the veil that rests over the head and the shoulders of the wearer is understood as a symbol of humble and obedient submission to God, and it testifies that the virgin is a bride of Christ.

Furthermore, the *PRG* describes the veiling rite thus:

> The benediction having been completed, and she having publicly professed concerning the observance of the sacred veil at the examination of the bishop, the bishop should put the veil upon the head of the virgin herself, saying: "Receive the sacred veil, maiden, that you may bear it without blemish before the tribunal of our Lord Jesus Christ, to whom every knee is bent of those that are in Heaven, on earth, and under the earth [cf. Phil 2:10]." Response: Amen.
>
> Then the veiled one herself begins the antiphon: "The Lord has clothed me in a robe woven from gold and has adorned me with immense jewels," with the other nuns who are present continuing. And if there shall have been several [maidens] veiled, the same antiphon should be begun by each separately as above.

---

corpore pariter, et animo incontaminato custodiant; ut quando ad perpetuam Sanctorum remunerationem venerit, cum prudentibus et ipsae Virginibus praeparatae, te perducente, ad sempiternae felicitatis nuptias introire mereantur. Qui vivis et regnas, Deus, per omnia saecula saeculorum. Amen.

Prayer after having taken the veil: "May the protection of your goodness preserve your maidservant, Lord, that her resolution of holy continence, which you inspiring, she has undertaken, she may preserve unharmed, you guiding [her]. Through our Lord Jesus Christ ... "

The antiphon follows: "I am espoused to him whom the angels serve, whose splendor the sun and the moon admire."

[Prayer:] "Grant, we beseech you, almighty God, that this your maidservant, who for the hope of eternal reward earnestly wishes to be consecrated to you, may persevere with faithfulness and her entire soul in her holy resolution. May you, almighty Father, vouchsafe to sanctify and bless and preserve her forever. Grant her humility, chastity, obedience, charity, and a multitude of all good works. Give her, O Lord, for her works, glory; for her purity, reverence; for her chastity, sanctity; that she may be able to attain to the merit of glory."

Thus we see that in the right spiritual context, in this case the consecration of virgins, the veil is not merely an article of clothing, but a sign of a deep and noble spiritual reality.

ST. THOMAS AQUINAS

In his commentary on 1 Cor 11:8–16, St. Thomas Aquinas gave two ways of interpreting the phrase "because of the angels" (*propter Angelos*): first, the word "angels" refers to the good angels who gather and celebrate the Eucharist with the Church; and secondly, the word "angels" may also be a metaphor for priests.

Then when he says, *because of the angels*, he gives a third reason, which is taken on the part of the angels, saying: *A woman ought to have a veil on her head because of the angels*. This can be understood in two ways: in one way about the heavenly angels who are believed to visit congregations of the faithful, especially when the sacred mysteries are celebrated. And therefore at that time women as well as men ought to present themselves honorably and ordinately as reverence to them, according to Ps 138 (v. 1): "Before the angels I sing thy praise." In another way it can be understood in the sense that priests are called angels, inasmuch as they proclaim divine things to the people according to Mal (2:7): "For the lips of a priest should guard knowledge, and men should seek instruction from his mouth; for he is the angel of the Lord of hosts." Therefore, the woman should always have a covering over her head because of the angels, i.e., the priests, for two reasons: first, as reverence toward them, to which it pertains that women should behave honorably before them. Hence it says in Sir (7:30): "With all your might love your maker and do not forsake his priests." Secondly, for their safety, lest the sight of a woman not veiled excite their concupiscence. Hence it says in Sir (9:5): "Do not look intently at a virgin, lest you stumble and incur penalties for her."[16]

---

[16] *Commentary on 1 Corinthians* 11:8–16, no. 613.

Thus, according to Aquinas, women need to veil especially during the celebration of the Sacraments, first to respect the heavenly angels who celebrate the Mass with the Church, and secondly, to reverence and protect the earthly angels (that is, the priests) from inordinate desire.

1917 CODE OF CANON LAW

The 1917 Code of Canon Law explicitly required women to cover their heads during the Holy Mass.

> Canon 1262. 1. It is desirable that, consistent with ancient discipline, women be separated from men in church. 2. Men, in a church or outside a church, while they are assisting at sacred rites, shall be bare-headed, unless the approved mores of the people or peculiar circumstances of things determine otherwise; women, however, shall have a covered head and be modestly dressed, especially when they approach the table of the Lord.

Readers who have attended the Traditional Latin Mass will know that women covering their heads is the norm. This is because the TLM continues the customs that were in place prior to the Second Vatican Council. The TLM was revived in the year 2007 by Pope Benedict XVI through his *Summorum Pontificum*, and the practice of head coverings became known again in younger generations.

1983 CODE OF CANON LAW

The 1983 Code does not include the above law, as it, along with many other provisions of the 1917

Code, was intentionally not incorporated into the new Code.[17]

> Canon 6. §1. When this Code goes into effect, the following are abrogated: 1° the Code of Canon Law promulgated in 1917; 2° other universal or particular laws contrary to the prescriptions of this Code, unless particular laws are otherwise expressly provided for; 3° any universal or particular penal laws whatsoever issued by the Apostolic See, unless they are contained in this Code; 4° other universal disciplinary laws dealing with a matter which is regulated *ex integro* by this Code. §2. To the extent that the Canons of this Code reproduce the former law, they are to be assessed in the light also of canonical tradition.

Thus, there is no longer any *canonical obligation* for women to wear a headcovering, including a veil or the mantilla.

The more critical among us may raise some questions. If the custom of veiling, especially in the context of worship, has long been part of Catholic tradition, is supported by the Church Fathers and reputed theologians, and was once explicitly obliged in Canon Law, why does the new Code no longer prescribe it? Why is there almost no recommendation about this practice in the modern age, except in recent times when the chapel veil is becoming widely adopted once again? Does this not seem like a break in a tradition as old as the Church herself? Further, is there a connection between this reality

---

[17] See Appendix 2.

and the general decline of reverence towards the Eucharist?

Those questions are really not easy to answer. Some associate the omission with the sexual revolution beginning in the 1920s and reborn in a more radical form in the 1960s, whose bitter fruits include radical feminism, the breaking of the relationship between men and women, and spite for traditional Christian values in society and in the family. Some others argue that the disappearance of veiling is "only" a symptom of a cultural shift due to modernization in all aspects of life, including in worship. Still others think that Holy Mother Church no longer desires to "babysit" her children, so some matters are handed over to the personal discernment of the faithful. As the questions are open to various answers, discussions, and reflections that go beyond the scope of this book, I shall not try here to offer a definitive response.

CONCLUSION

Veiling is not a custom foreign to Catholic tradition. Its usage is mentioned in Scripture, it was recommended by Church Fathers and Doctors, and it was once a requirement according to the 1917 Code of Canon Law. The development of the teaching on veiling according to several Church Fathers and St. Thomas Aquinas is summarized in Table 2.

Although veiling during Mass is no longer a canonical obligation, we can see, from authoritative teaching and universal usage over many centuries that this practice is very good and worthy to be revived as a form of private devotion.

TABLE 2. SUMMARY OF TEACHINGS ON CHRISTIAN VEILING

	SCOPE	TIME	REASON
ST. JOHN CHRYSOSTOM	All the hair	All the time	*Theological:* "because of the angels" *Moral:* to prevent lust
ST. AMBROSE	All the hair	All the time	*Moral:* to prevent lust
ST. AUGUSTINE	All the hair	All the time	*Moral:* to encourage chastity
ST. THOMAS AQUINAS	Not mentioned	All the time, esp. during the celebration of the Sacraments	*Theological:* "because of the angels"; priests as angels *Moral:* to reverence priests and protect them from lust

Tiempo Orando
Fortunino Matania (1881-1963)

CHAPTER 2

The Bride Preparing Herself for the Wedding

MANTILLA IN THE HOLY MASS

Jesus had said in one of his parables: "The kingdom of heaven may be compared to a king who gave a marriage feast for his son" (Mt 22:2). The Eucharist is the sacramental anticipation and, in a certain sense, a "foretaste" of that royal feast which the Book of Revelation calls "the marriage supper of the Lamb" (cf. Rev 19:9). The bridegroom who is at the center of that marriage feast and of its Eucharistic foreshadowing and anticipation is the Lamb who "took away the sins of the world," the Redeemer.

—John Paul II [1]

*I*N ORDER TO understand why the mantilla only makes sense before the Blessed Sacrament, especially in the Holy Mass, first we have to understand the analogy of the Mass as a wedding feast.

In the parable of the wedding feast found in the Gospel of Matthew, we learn that love—spousal love,

---

[1] General Audience, September 13, 1989.

to be more specific — is a character of the Kingdom of God. In Matthew 22:2, the son of the king is the bridegroom, the future husband, and he is none other than Christ Himself. Christ establishes the Father's new covenant with humanity through a communion of love. The wedding feast is therefore an expression of this communion. Pope John Paul II said, "It is not difficult to see in this wedding feast a reference to the Eucharist: the sacrament of the new and eternal covenant, the sacrament of the marriage of Christ and humanity in the Church."[2]

Next we read that not everyone responds to the invitation. Even those who do still have to wear the proper wedding garments, because if not, they will be cast "into the darkness outside." The wedding garment is understood as the state of grace, a state when sanctifying grace is in us (cf. *Catechism of the Catholic Church* [CCC] 1861). The loss of sanctifying grace occurs when one is in a state of mortal sin, and mortal sin can be absolved only through the Sacrament of Penance. "By the same charity that it enkindles in us, the Eucharist preserves us from future mortal sins. The more we share the life of Christ and progress in his friendship, the more difficult it is to break away from him by mortal sin. The Eucharist is not ordered to the forgiveness of mortal sins — that is proper to the sacrament of Reconciliation. The Eucharist is properly the sacrament of those who are in full communion with the Church" (CCC 1395).

Therefore, the proper "wedding garment" to receive Holy Communion (a word that comes from *communio*, which means fellowship) is the grace of a

---

[2] General Audience, September 18, 1991.

soul free from mortal sin. Those who attend the feast without a wedding garment — that is, without grace, or without recovering lost sanctifying grace by a sincere confession prior to receiving Communion — will invite punishment upon themselves (cf. Mt 22:12; 1 Cor 11:27-30). The Sacrament of the Eucharist is a medicine for the sick still alive, but the dead (i.e., spiritually dead) must first be resurrected through the Sacrament of Penance.

The beautiful and bridal-looking mantilla symbolizes a pure bride who is ready both bodily and spiritually to welcome her Bridegroom. On earth, our Bridegroom is hidden under the form of a small piece of bread. Receiving Holy Communion is a foretaste of the heavenly wedding feast as explained by Pope John Paul II. Just as the soul in a state of grace receives Communion on earth, so the spotless Bride of Christ will later receive in heaven her Bridegroom, who has loved her first (cf. 1 John 4:19).

The mantilla is the veil of the Bride of Christ. While it is a sign of the Church's holiness (see chapter 1), at the same time it personally reminds the wearer that, as an image of the Church, she is called to a holy life, one more appropriate to the image of a faithful bride. How fortunate it is for women to be allowed to become an image of Christ's own Bride! Therefore, the mantilla must not become merely a fashion item, but it must truly be a physical sign of that spiritual wedding garment. And because of this, wearing the mantilla without other spiritual disciplines is not enough (see chapter 6).

Thus the Holy Mass is seen as a heavenly wedding feast. Blessed are those who have been called to the wedding feast of the Lamb! So we ought to be grateful for the invitation by adorning ourselves as beautifully as we can, through physical modesty and a spiritual state of grace, in order to enter into the glorious communion of love. The Church is indeed composed of men and women, but in their feminine nature women manifest more clearly the image of the Bride of Christ.[3] By wearing the mantilla during the Holy Mass, a woman not only asserts the meaning of the mantilla (as the preceding chapter explained it), but also affirms the reality of the mystical marriage and preaches it to her neighbors.

---

[3] For an extensive treatment of the irreducible perfections of male and female humanity as they relate to the Gospel and the liturgy, see Peter Kwasniewski, *Ministers of Christ: Recovering the Roles of Clergy and Laity in an Age of Confusion* (Manchester, NH: Crisis Publications, 2021), esp. ix–xxv, 13–40, 103–15, 173–202.

The Return from Mass, Valencia, Spain
Francisco Gras (1878-?)

Rezando en la iglesia
José Gallegos y Arnosa (1857-1917)

CHAPTER 3

Why Wear the Mantilla in Modern Times

*W*E HAVE now understood the history and doctrine of Christian veiling. In modern times, the veil, particularly the mantilla, is still commonly worn in certain countries, such as South Korea and Spain. In recent years, the mantilla has started making a comeback all across the world. Although the traditional reasons for veiling exist and deserve to be studied and contemplated (see chapters 1 and 2), the mantilla today is full of new meaning for women who long to love Christ more deeply.

REASON 1: HUMILITY AND REVERENCE BEFORE THE BLESSED SACRAMENT

This is the main reason why modern women take up the mantilla once again. As a form of devotion, the mantilla is a Eucharistic devotion, which means it is specifically centered on Christ in the Blessed Sacrament. Rebekah veiled herself in the presence of her future husband Isaac; modern women veil themselves in the presence of their Heavenly Spouse.

St. Paul said that the woman's hair is her "honor"
(1 Cor 11:15). Even secular society is aware of it:
in shampoo commercials on television, it is not
uncommon to hear a woman's hair referred to as
her "crown." Yet, we have never heard of male hair
being called that. Moreover, throughout history, men
who want to look more authoritative usually wear
a head covering such as a top hat, cap, blangkon,
or turban. This is why the opposite rule applies to
men: men have to be bare-headed before the Blessed
Sacrament to show their *masculine* humility.

But the woman's hair, indeed it is her crown and
her beauty! Thus, in the face of the Most Glorious
Sacrament, we are called to be present in a modest
manner by veiling our own "crown." We want to
say, with the cousin of the Lord, "He must increase,
but I must decrease" (John 3:30). So, a woman veils
herself so that all glory is given to God, not to herself.

REASON 2: THE IMAGE OF WOMAN AS A SACRED
VESSEL

We see how the sacred vessels containing the
Body and Blood of the Lord are always veiled or
covered. In the past, the Holy of Holies in the temple
containing the Ark of the Covenant was separated
from the other parts of the building with a long
and heavy curtain. Now, we see how the Body of
the Lord is "hidden" inside the tabernacle, which is
veiled by a white curtain. And of course, the cibo-
rium and the chalice are also veiled, and the veil is
lifted only when the priest is about to consecrate
the bread and wine.

A woman shares this role as a sacred vessel.
Like the tabernacle containing Life itself, women

are endowed with the ability to conceive and give birth to a new human life. Even nature proclaims this truth: the woman's uterus is shaped like a cup or a chalice. Therefore, just as the sacred vessels of the Church are veiled, so the woman dresses and veils herself accordingly. This symbolism helps a woman to realize and maintain her purity more firmly.

REASON 3: THE IMAGE OF WOMAN AS THE BRIDE OF CHRIST

The Church is the Bride of Christ, and the woman is the image of the Church (see chapter 1), therefore the woman is the image of the Bride of Christ. The form of the mantilla itself is like a bridal veil, so the woman wearing it rightly feels like a bride. The mantilla's bridal characteristics continually remind women to always behave, think, speak, and dress like a bride. Clearly, this does not mean that a woman should be dressed in a long white wedding gown every day, but her attitude should reflect an understanding that she was created, sanctified, blessed, and loved in a special way by a Lover unmatched by anyone, and Who is always faithful in waiting for her to come to the eternal wedding feast in heaven. Wearing a mantilla is an excellent way to instill this appreciation.

REASON 4: THE MANTILLA IS A UNIQUELY FEMININE DEVOTION

Obviously, only women wear the mantilla. This fact endows the practice with special appeal, because now women can express their love for their Heavenly Spouse in a special way, a feminine way, which cannot be imitated by men. Men and women are created differently and they are meant to worship God in different ways according to their sexuality. In a society that tries to obliterate or relativize sexual difference, *everyone* suffers loss: we lose ways of acting and reacting, of being and giving, that are fine-tuned to our sex.

REASON 5: THE MANTILLA EXPRESSES TRUE FEMININITY

In his *Theology of the Body* audiences, Pope John Paul II taught that gender (or, more properly, sex) is an ontological concept, meaning it is related to the essence of a person. A person's sex is not merely a matter of physical sexual organs; it also encompasses the identity of a person, it contributes to determining "who" he or she is. In other words, being male and being female are two different ways of being human, and each one is irreplaceable. "Gender does not only determine the somatic individuality of man, but also determines his personal identity and concreteness."[1] Elsewhere, he asserts that masculinity only makes sense if there is femininity, and femininity only makes sense if there is masculinity.

> Let us recall the passage of Genesis 2:23: "Then the man said, This is now bone of my bones and flesh of my flesh. She will be called woman, because she was taken out of man." In the light of this passage, we understand that knowledge of man passes through masculinity and femininity. These are, as it were, two "incarnations" of the same metaphysical solitude before God and the world—they are two ways of "being a body" and at the same time a human being, which complement each other.... As shown by

---

[1] John Paul II, *Theology of the Body* 20.5.

> Genesis 2:23, femininity finds herself in the presence of masculinity, while masculinity is confirmed through femininity.[2]

True femininity as understood through John Paul II's theology of the body is very different from the doctrine of radical feminism, which compels women to become men, as if they should be the same as men.

The devotion of the mantilla, because of its very feminine characteristics (see Reason 4), reaffirms these essential differences between man and woman. When a woman wears a mantilla over her head, she sets herself apart from men. Through the mantilla, Catholic women are reminded to embrace their feminine identity that is unrepeatable and irreplaceable, and to worship God as a female human being with all her femaleness. This is a witness that confounds modern feminist culture.

REASON 6: THE MANTILLA INCREASES AWARENESS OF MODESTY OF CLOTHING

It is true that with or without a mantilla, women should always dress decently for Mass. But we realize that our natural inclination to sin often obscures or even shuts down our judgment. Intellectually we might understand what the Mass is all about—the celebration of the Holy Sacrifice of Christ, a sacred celebration in which the Lord is truly present in Body, Blood, Soul, and Divinity. The Mass is what happens when heaven descends down and kisses the earth. But, in fact, we may not be immediately aware of the logical consequences, for our body, of such a sublime understanding.

---

2 John Paul II, *Theology of the Body* 10.1.

The mantilla can be considered a tool to discipline the body. It is worn only in the context of worship. Once we drape it over our heads, psychologically we will immediately feel "different." As the body affects the spirit, so the spirit also affects the body: we would feel "less suitable" when matching the mantilla with clothes that are too casual or too vulgar. Gradually, the habit of wearing the mantilla will affect our choice of clothing for church; it might even affect our choice of dress in general. I can personally testify to this because I have experienced it myself.

REASON 7: THE MANTILLA INCREASES SENSITIVITY TOWARDS SACRED SPACE AND TIME

The Holy Mass is not just any religious service. When we set foot inside a Catholic church building where the Blessed Sacrament is enthroned, we enter "another world," a world of sacred space and time, because the Real Presence of Christ is there. With the right externals, we help reorient or "redirect" our inner disposition to the correct focus, which cannot always be discerned by our senses. The mantilla symbolically motivates the woman to bow her head in prayer, to look down humbly under the gaze of God who is beautifully and mysteriously hidden in the Blessed Sacrament. With head bowed, she not only worships God in front of her, but also worships Him in her own interior castle.

REASON 8: THE MANTILLA IS A SIGN OF REBELLION

In its own way, the mantilla can become a "rebellion" against the culture of disobedience. Modern culture has been saturated by a *non serviam* attitude,

"I will not serve." Obedience to a higher authority may have become a foreign concept; where it exists it looks odd. The humble mantilla is a symbol and a reminder of radical obedience and submission to an authority, namely the authority of Christ. A woman who dares to wear modest attire in obedience to her Lord is rebelling against an arrogant and selfish "me" culture.

REASON 9: MANTILLA AND THE EXAMPLE OF MARY

A woman wearing the mantilla would be reminded of the noblest of all creatures, the Blessed Virgin Mary, Mother of God. No one on earth can love Jesus more than the Virgin Mary. Her humility and love rise like fragrant incense before God. The veil of the Virgin Mary signifies her purity and simplicity, her humble and trustful surrender to God.

Women who love Christ need to be aware of their resemblance to the Blessed Virgin when wearing a mantilla. Mary is the most ideal icon or image of the Church. Hopefully, women will be increasingly compelled to imitate Our Lady in her purity, simplicity, humility, and love, and ultimately, her sanctity.

In Träumen versunken
Friedrich von Amerling (1803–1887)

CHAPTER 4

Responses to Common Objections Against the Mantilla

LTHOUGH there are overwhelming historical, theological, and psychological reasons to support the mantilla, there are still many who oppose this traditional devotion. Personally, I believe that those who question or object to this practice do so not out of malice, but out of ignorance, due to the lack of catechesis on the subject matter. On the other hand, the courage and sacrifice made by women who faithfully veil for the Lord must be commended.

In this chapter, I will give some of the most frequent objections raised about mantilla. The responses to these objections are also included, with the hope that women who veil can grow in their appreciation of the devotion and acquire the means for explaining it to others.

OBJECTION 1: THE MANTILLA IS NO LONGER A REQUIREMENT

The Catholic faith has binding rules on basic and fundamental dogmas that must be believed by anyone who calls himself a Catholic. However, there are a lot more things that are not required but still encouraged. For example, the Church mandates fasting and abstinence during Lent and abstinence of meat on Fridays throughout the year. But are fasting and abstinence forbidden outside of these times? Of course not! They are allowed, and are highly praiseworthy when practiced in the correct way and with the right intention, for example, to exercise self-control or improve the quality of prayer.

Since the 1983 Code, veiling is not mandatory, but it does not mean it can be underestimated or dismissed as a useless "product of the past."

What, then, is the basis of the use of the mantilla today?

Love. Yes, love is the basis of this devotion in modern times. True love would not stand just doing the bare minimum; it will try to do more and more. "Love looks to the eternal,"[1] hence the desire to always give more and give better is actually a human effort, finite and limited, to get closer to the infinite and eternal. Veiling before the Blessed Sacrament is one way to love Christ with an "extra," beyond the minimum limits specified by the Church.

OBJECTION 2: THE MANTILLA IS A CUSTOM FROM THE OLD MASS; THERE IS NO SUCH THING IN THE NEW MASS

It is true that the custom of wearing the mantilla is an inheritance of the Traditional Latin Mass. I also got introduced to the mantilla from a Latin Mass I attended about five years ago. But here is the simple logic: if we wear the mantilla in reverence to Christ, and we believe that the Christ whom we worship

---

[1] Benedict XVI, *Deus Caritas Est*, no. 6.

and whose Body and Blood we consume is the same Christ whether in the TLM ("old Mass") or in the Novus Ordo Mass ("new Mass"), then shouldn't we treat Him just the same regardless of the forms of the Mass? Why are we willing to respect Him with the mantilla in the TLM but not in the Novus Ordo?

Admittedly, there is a bad tendency to be "more casual" in the way we understand and treat the Holy Victim in the Novus Ordo Mass. We have to avoid this casual and subjective attitude as best we can, because there is no love story more grave and more real than the glorious Lord emptying Himself to become food for lowly man. Wearing the mantilla every time we stand before the Blessed Sacrament, whatever form of the Mass it is, preaches an acknowledgment that Christ is the same yesterday, today, and forever (cf. Heb 13:8).

OBJECTION 3: NO NEED TO VEIL, SINCE GOD LOOKS AT THE HEART

The argument "God looks at the heart" is so often heard when discussing external expressions of faith. Studying the Catholic faith? Oh, faith does not need to be debated; the heart is what is important. Trying to do the liturgy properly? But the Lord looks at the heart, why bother being liturgically correct but wicked at heart! Wearing the mantilla? No need, because God looks at the heart.

We must be careful not to use the Scripture as a justification of personal laziness. Saying "God looks at the heart" or "the heart is what is important" could end up treating the soul and the body as two separate entities that do not affect each other, as if pure and earnest desires will not materialise through word and deed. This argument sounds so simple, but it shows a rather dangerous understanding of the faith, so it needs to be addressed more seriously.

Indeed, people often do things that contradict themselves. For example, one's speech does not always reflect one's thoughts or deeds, and vice versa. It is one of the four wounds of original sin, namely the loss of integrity.[2] But do we really want to live in this condition? Do we not want to continually improve ourselves to be more like God's plan for man in the beginning? The body and the soul, the heart and the will must go hand in hand, driven by love, because this is what God originally intended.

But if so, where does the idea "God looks at the heart" come from? It seems that these words are taken from either 1 Samuel 16:7 or Jeremiah 17:10. To avoid understanding them out of context, the longer texts are presented here.

> As they came, he looked at Eliab and thought,
> "Surely the anointed is here before the Lord."
> But the Lord said to Samuel: Do not judge
> from his appearance or from his lofty stature,

---

2 Church Tradition teaches that our First Parents were blessed with one supernatural gift and three preternatural gifts. The preternatural gift is sanctifying grace that gives us original righteousness. The preternatural gifts are the three I's: immortality (which also includes impassibility), integrity, and infused knowledge. With these four gifts, man is truly an *Imago Dei*. Due to sin, however, man lost these gifts and fell into the natural state bearing the four "wounds": original sin (the loss of sanctifying grace and original righteousness), ignorance (loss of infused knowledge), concupiscence (loss of reason's control over passion), and disease and death (loss of immortality) (see *ST* Ia-IIae, Q. 85, art. 3). Concupiscence represents disintegrity; man in his natural state finds it much more difficult to harmonize passion and reason, and this is apparent through, for instance, inconsistency or disharmony between belief, thought, deeds, and speech.

> because I have rejected him. God does not
> see as a mortal, who sees the appearance. The
> Lord looks into the heart. (1 Sam 16: 6–7)
>
> Thus says the Lord: Cursed is the man who
> trusts in human beings, who makes flesh his
> strength, whose heart turns away from the
> Lord. He is like a barren bush in the waste-
> land that enjoys no change of season, but
> stands in lava beds in the wilderness, a land,
> salty and uninhabited. Blessed are those who
> trust in the Lord, the Lord will be their trust.
> They are like a tree planted beside the waters
> that stretches out its roots to the stream: It
> does not fear heat when it comes, its leaves
> stay green; in the year of drought it shows
> no distress, but still produces fruit. More
> tortuous than anything is the human heart,
> beyond remedy; who can understand it? I,
> the Lord, explore the mind and test the heart,
> giving to all according to their ways, accord-
> ing to the fruit of their deeds. (Jer 17: 5–10)

The first passage is part of the story of the prophet Samuel, who was looking for someone who deserved to be anointed as a king of Israel. Samuel, naturally, was first interested in gallant-looking youths, but God's chosen king was David, the young shepherd. Meanwhile, the second passage speaks of a warning to always rely on God, not on oneself or one's fellow human beings.

Neither passage contrasts the heart and the deeds, or love and the expressions of love. In fact, the second passage warns that we should not be so trusting of the human heart. It says that "more tortuous than anything is the human heart." Original sin has dam-aged the human heart, making it more corrupt and more inclined towards evil.

"The important thing is the heart": this may be true, as long as the heart is purified, with the Sacrament of the Eucharist, the Sacrament of Confession, and lifelong penances. The pure and loving heart surely will not remain silent. Because a human has a body and a soul, and the heart and the will, the spirit will move the body, and the heart will move the will.

OBJECTION 4: NO NEED TO VEIL, SINCE I LOVE GOD WITH ALL MY HEART

What does the Law of Love say? "You shall love the Lord, your God, with all your heart, with all your being, with all your strength, and with all your mind, and your neighbor as yourself." (Lk 10:27; Mt 22:37). He never says: "Love God with your heart only." No, He demands that we love Him with all our *hearts*, all our *souls*, all our *strength*, and all our *minds*. The love that is felt in the heart will encourage a person to do something *bodily* for the sake of the beloved. There is no need for special spiritual understanding on this matter, because we can see it in the love between parents and children, between lovers, between friends, between a teacher and his students, and so on. It was love that "moved" God to become man and die on the cross for the sake of mankind whom He so loved.

Veiling is just one small and simple way for a woman to meet the high demands of love. As noted by many women who veil (see chapter 7), the mantilla requires readiness throughout, and in turn, the mantilla changes them in subtle ways.

OBJECTION 5: THE MANTILLA IS AN OLD TRADITION, BUT THE CHURCH MUST KEEP WITH THE TIMES

The Church is the Bride of Christ; just like her

Lover, She is "ever ancient, ever new" (St. Augustine, *Confessions*). The Church is an institution that preserves tradition. Paying homage to saints is one example of the Church's appreciation to her predecessors and an acknowledgment of the work of God among men.

It is true that times have changed and they continue to evolve. Many traditions, scientific views, and old beliefs are no longer relevant today, have been proven wrong, or need an updating. But that does not mean that we should follow the times in every respect, because not all that is new is good or right, or always "more" than the past. The mantilla brings with itself perennial values that are timeless and must be upheld at all times; these values include proper reverence to God, purity, order, modesty, humility, the struggle for holiness, and the dignity and mystery of woman. If these all sound strange, heavy, or radical, and consequently the mantilla is considered countercultural, it is not because the values are wrong, but because the culture of this age has undergone much perversion.

In *Mere Christianity*, C. S. Lewis wrote how genuine progress does not always mean a forward step:

> We all want progress. But progress means getting closer to where we want to be. And when you have taken a wrong turn, it will not make you move closer [the goal]. If you are on the wrong road, progress means doing an about-turn and walking back to the right road; and in that case the man who turns back sooner is the most progressive man.

OBJECTION 6: THE MANTILLA MAKES A CATHOLIC WOMAN LOOK LIKE A MUSLIM WOMAN

This lazy objection equates Catholic veiling with the Islamic dresscode, ignoring the fact that veiling at

prayer is also practiced by Jewish and Eastern Orthodox communities, among many others. The mantilla
differs from the Muslim veil in obvious ways. As a
Eucharistic devotion, Catholic women wear the mantilla only when they are in the presence of the Blessed
Sacrament, whether in the Mass, Adoration, or other
prayer in church. In addition, it is also clear that the
physical shape of the mantilla is very different from
the Muslim hijab. According to my personal experience as described in the Preface, the mantilla may
even become a gateway to preach the Catholic faith
and traditions, not just to fellow Catholics, but also
to people of other creeds. In this sense, veiling may be
regarded as providing a common ground in conversa-
tions about modesty of dress and the role of women
in the religious context.

OBJECTION 7: THE MANTILLA IS JUST A TREND

Yes, it could be so, if it is not accompanied with
good catechesis about the Eucharist, true femininity,
and the mantilla itself. That is the purpose of this
book: the hope is that, with the growing understanding of theology and spirituality behind the mantilla,
wearers and non-wearers alike will be moved to
preserve this meaningful and beautiful tradition.

OBJECTION 8: VEILING IS "HOLIER-THAN-THOU"

If veiling is sanctimonious, then the rosary, the
scapular, and the devotion to the Divine Mercy
are sanctimonious too. A devotion is practiced not
because the devotee feels holy, but precisely because
he or she is far from holiness and therefore needs
help to get closer to and more intimate with God.
The mantilla disciplines the mind through disciplining

the body, so the women who wear it will more easily enter into communion with the Heavenly Beloved. As St. Francis de Sales counsels:

> In short, devotion is nothing but that spiritual agility and vivacity, by which charity works in us, or we by her, with alacrity and affection; and as it is the business of charity to make us observe all God's commandments generally and without exception, so it is the part of devotion to make us observe them cheerfully and with diligence.... As devotion, then, consists in a certain excellent degree of charity, it makes us not only active and diligent in the observance of God's commandments, but it also excites us to the performance of every good work with an affectionate alacrity, not commanded, indeed, but only counselled.[3]

OBJECTION 9: THE MANTILLA ATTRACTS ATTENTION

Indeed, we should not veil deliberately to attract attention. At the same time, however, the mantilla is a visual, public sign saying that "the Lord is present in the tabernacle, He is the God we worship, we love, and we obey."

For women who veil, let us ponder these questions every day and pray about them: What's my motivation? Do I purposely want to seek the attention of others, or do I really want to love and respect God?

The mantilla is a testimony, just as a nun's habit, a priest's cassock, or a wedding ring is a testimony. Each one of them does make the wearer look different and might attract attention. But we are called to be

---

3 St. Francis de Sales, *Introduction to the Devout Life*, Part I, ch. 2.

salt and light of the world (cf. Mt 5: 13–16); if the salt has lost its saltiness and is just the same as the food it's supposed to salt, what good is that salt? Being salt and light indeed makes someone "different," "countercultural," even "visible" in a positive sense; as long as these are just side effects and do not become the purpose of our devotion, let us humbly admit it, accept it, and be grateful for it, because we have been allowed to take part in the Divine Light.

OBJECTION 10: THE MANTILLA IS THE "COSTUME" OF CERTAIN GROUPS

These days, I often see mantillas being worn by female members of choirs or specialized groups. On the one hand, I am grateful that women are discovering this beautiful tradition. These communities may be heralds of the return of Catholic veiling. On the other hand, I have to admit that this particular objection is valid; I myself am concerned that some people consider the mantilla as a "costume" of certain groups, and consequently they associate it with exclusivity or elitism.

Let me reassert here: the mantilla is a devotion to the Blessed Sacrament; in other words, it is a Eucharistic devotion, even a liturgical one. Therefore, it is right and just that the mantilla should be worn according to its meaning and its purpose, that is, every time the wearer is before the Blessed Sacrament. If, for instance, all female members of the choir are asked by their leader to wear the mantilla when they are singing at Mass, then this may be justified, as long as it is motivated by a desire to increase reverence towards the hidden God. However, if the mantilla is made into part of the "uniform" of that choir group, and consequently the mantilla is also worn outside of Mass, such as in a choir competition in an ordinary room, then this is a degradation of the real meaning of the mantilla by blurring it and replacing it with a new, incorrect association.

Likewise, other groups and communities that require the mantilla for their women should use the sacred veil according to the right time and the right place as explained above. What needs to be carefully considered is the motivation. Let all mantilla wearers, including those in groups and communities, ask themselves whether they wear the veil for Christ in a sacred place and time, or for their own exclusive identity.

OBJECTION 11: CLOTHING IS NOT RELATED TO SPIRITUALITY

To this objection, St. Thomas Aquinas already wrote a response. First, he outlines three vices related to outward dress:

> Honesty pertains to virtue. Now a certain honesty is observed in the outward apparel.... In point of excess, this inordinate attachment occurs in three ways. First, when a man seeks glory from excessive attention to dress; in so far as dress and such like things are a kind of ornament.... Secondly, when a man seeks sensuous pleasure from excessive attention to dress, in so far as dress is directed to the body's comfort. Thirdly, when a man is too solicitous in his attention to outward apparel....

Then, he contrasts three virtues with these three vices:

> Andronicus reckons three virtues in connection with outward attire: "humility," which excludes the seeking of glory, wherefore he says that humility is "the habit of avoiding

excessive expenditure and parade"; "contentment," which excludes the seeking of sensuous pleasure, wherefore he says that "contentedness is the habit that makes a man satisfied with what is suitable, and enables him to determine what is becoming in his manner of life" (according to the saying of the Apostle, 1 Timothy 6:8, "Having food and wherewith to be covered, with these let us be content"); and "simplicity," which excludes excessive solicitude about such things, wherefore he says that "simplicity is a habit that makes a man contented with what he has." ... Although outward attire does not come from nature, it belongs to natural reason to moderate it; so that we are naturally inclined to be the recipients of the virtue that moderates outward raiment.[4]

Aquinas taught that outer garments are associated with virtue and vice, which in turn are related to spirituality. The virtues include humility, a sense of sufficiency, and simplicity. It is not the apparel itself that brings spiritual virtues; it is rather how we use it, the purpose of its usage, and how we control it that are an exercise of reason and self-discipline, and these things lead to virtues.

However, Aquinas also warns that in some cases, physical simplicity can be an impropriety if worn on the wrong occasions, and even become a sin if tainted with superstition (note that Aquinas's notion of superstition is different from the typical meaning of that word today; for him it means "a vice opposed to the virtue of religion by way of excess").

---

[4] *Summa theologiae* II-II, Q. 169, art. 1.

> Those who are placed in a position of dignity,
> or again the ministers of the altar, are attired
> in more costly apparel than others, not for
> the sake of their own glory, but to indicate
> the excellence of their office or of the divine
> worship: wherefore this is not sinful in
> them.... Likewise there may be sin on the
> part of deficiency: although it is not always a
> sin to wear coarser clothes than other people.
> For, if this be done through ostentation or
> pride, in order to set oneself above others,
> it is a sin of superstition; whereas, if this
> be done to tame the flesh, or to humble the
> spirit, it belongs to the virtue of temperance.[5]

Indeed, the clothes themselves do not completely
determine one's spirituality or piety. However, spiritual life and a good internal disposition will inevitably
radiate out through the choice of clothing, and how
one wears it. The "right" clothes will help educate the
body and soul. A simple proof that what we do to the
body affects the soul is to recall the many times we
say that "this outfit makes me feel uncomfortable" or
"this dress makes me feel more confident."

Therefore, a piece of cloth like a mantilla, too,
when worn with faith, self-control, and the correct intention, as well as overall harmonious fashion,
makes the wearer able to develop her spirituality. In
addition, the lace mantilla is beautiful, which makes
it appropriate to be worn in the presence of the King
of kings. Here let us remember the advice of Benedict
XVI: "Everything related to the Eucharist should be
marked by beauty."[6]

---

5 Ibid., ad 2.
6 Benedict XVI, *Sacramentum Caritatis*, no. 41.

Portrait of a Young Girl Wearing a White Veil
Alexei Harlamoff (1840–1925)

CHAPTER 5

Rules and Practical Tips for Wearing the Mantilla

RE THERE SPEcial rules for wearing a mantilla?

The traditional rule is: a white veil for single women, and a black veil for married or widowed women. Additionally, to this day, the veil is compulsory for women who are meeting the Pope in a private audience; a black veil is worn by all women, except for queens or wives of kings of Catholic kingdoms, who are permitted to wear a white veil. However, with the changing of times, and the loss (for a time) of the custom of veiling, the once strong connection between color and state in life has largely vanished. Today, a wide variety of mantillas and veils are sold in online stores, in many colors, shapes, and patterns, though they all still maintain elegance and simplicity.

WHEN DO WE WEAR THE MANTILLA?

This question is very important because it is so frequently asked. If readers have read at least

Chapters 2 and 3 of this book, then the answer
should already be clear: the mantilla, as a Eucharistic devotion, *is most properly worn before the Blessed
Sacrament,* for example during Mass and Eucharistic
Adoration. The mantilla, the veil of the Bride of
Christ, radiates its truest and most sensible meaning
when worn in front of the Heavenly Bridegroom.

But what about other instances, such as private
prayer at home, prayer at a Marian grotto, confession, Divine Office outside a sacred space, and
so on? Some women do wear the mantilla during
confession, arguing that the priest is acting in the
person of Christ (*in persona Christi*). Some others
wear the mantilla in other prayer sessions; these
women very likely consider the mantilla as another
"instrument to aid prayer." Are these reasons right
or wrong?

There is really no black-and-white rule regarding the matter. The measurement used here should
be one of the three qualities of objective beauty
according to St. Thomas Aquinas, that is, *consonan-
tia* or due proportion or harmony (the other two
characteristics being *integritas* or integrity, and *claritas*
or clarity).

Something that possesses the quality of *conso-
nantia* means it is in harmony with order, with its
essence, with its final end or purpose. Harmony
concerns a gradual spectrum, not an all-or-nothing
alternative. Hence, the appropriate question to pose
is not whether it is right or wrong, but whether
it is harmonious or disharmonious, and to what
extent. Applied to the question "When do we wear
the mantilla?," the following table suggests how we
might respond:

TABLE 3: WHEN DO WE WEAR THE MANTILLA?

LEAST HARMONIOUS

→

Occasions outside a sacred space, esp. secular events, e.g. choir competition in a concert hall, community events in an ordinary room.

Private or group prayers not in the same room with the Blessed Sacrament, e.g. Divine Office or *lectio* in a meeting room, rosary at an outdoor Marian shrine, Bible study at home.

Confession, esp. when done inside a proper church confessional.

MOST HARMONIOUS

→

- Holy Mass
- Adoration / Holy Hour
- Procession of the Blessed Sacrament
- Other prayers before the Blessed Sacrament

COLOR

In South Korea, women generally only wear white mantillas, regardless of whether they are single or married. In other countries, many women still faithfully follow the traditional rule of color as mentioned before. But many also adjust the colors of their veils according to the liturgical calendar: white or other bright colors for the whole year, except during Advent and Lent where black or other dark veils are worn.

SHAPE

Traditional mantillas are triangular or semi-circular, and they generally fall slightly below the shoulder when worn. But now there are also large rectangular mantillas and "infinity"-shaped veils. Mantillas for children are often added with a pair of small ribbons at the two ends of the front side, so they can be fastened under the chin to prevent the mantilla from slipping off of an active child's head.

MATERIAL

The mantilla is usually made of lace, but can also be made from other types of fabric, such as knitted fabrics. For reasons of practicality, the material should be heavy enough to drape well when worn and to reduce the frequency of slipping off.

PATTERNS

Mantillas usually bear floral patterns — small, medium, or large-sized, either covering the entire surface of the mantilla, or on certain parts only. The edge is often trimmed with a scalloped cut. There are mantillas made of plain white cloth instead of lace. The image of the Virgin Mary or a small cross is sometimes added.

WHAT IF THE MANTILLA SLIPS OFF?

Women with straight and silky hair often complain about their veils slipping off so easily. To avoid this, a hair pin or small comb can be sewn or glued on the inside of the mantilla. For children, the mantilla can be fastened with a clear or white headband, or a pair of ribbons can be added so it can be fastened under the chin. Some mantilla online shops sell a comb separately or already sewn or glued to the mantilla. Alternatively, women may use a mantilla with longer ends (such as the rectangular-shaped ones) or infinity veils.

BUT I DON'T HAVE A MANTILLA!

You are interested in veiling but do not have a mantilla? Maybe you cannot buy one online, or you cannot or do not have time to make your own — in this case, start with other head coverings, such as a thin shawl or scarf, a pashmina, or a large headband tied behind the neck.

DOES A MANTILLA HAVE TO BE BLESSED FIRST?

It is not necessary, but it is certainly a good practice. Keep in mind that a mantilla that has been blessed must be treated more respectfully. When a blessing is conveyed upon an ordinary veil, not a mantilla, that veil should be used only for Mass and prayer, not for ordinary or secular events.

STORAGE FOR THE MANTILLA

Based on my personal experience, the best container for the mantilla is a drawstring cloth pouch. Such pouches are safest especially for lace mantillas, which are prone to get tangled in a zipper or attached to velcro. For other veils not made of lace, storage options are more variable.

I WANT TO TRY MAKING MY OWN MANTILLA. WHAT IS THE SHAPE AND WHAT ARE THE MEASUREMENTS?

A "classic" mantilla is triangular, with its two front ends (the two "feet" of the triangle) falling in front of the shoulders. The "peak" of the triangle falls on the back of the neck or on the upper back, depending on its length. The size of the mantilla may be modified to preference. A mantilla can also be semicircular or D-shaped, rectangular, or loop-shaped ("infinity veil").

The following are some examples of the shapes and measurements of various mantillas from my small collection.

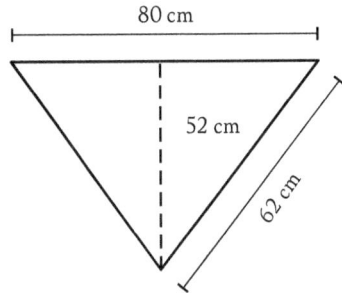

CLASSIC TRIANGLE, SMALL
(the lower edge falls slightly above the shoulders)

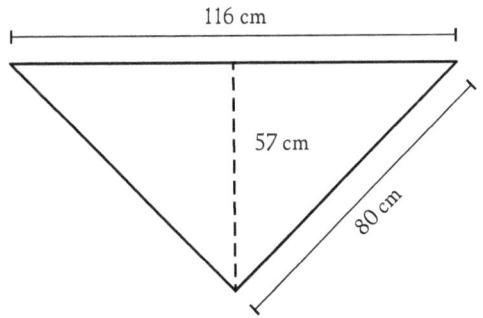

CLASSIC TRIANGLE, MEDIUM
(the lower edge falls slightly below the shoulders)

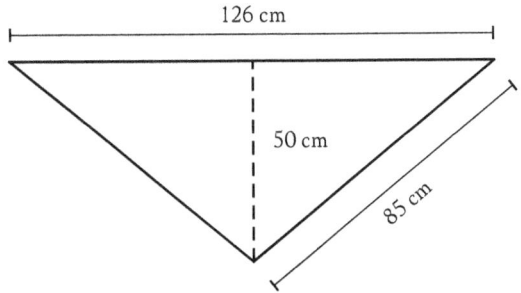

CLASSIC TRIANGLE, LARGE
(the lower edge covers most of the shoulders
and upper back)

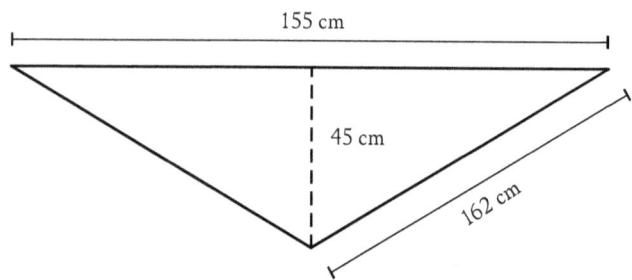

LONG TRIANGLE

The proportion of this particular veil is somewhat different from the classic triangular form. Here, the "peak" of the triangle which falls on the back of the head is much shorter compared to its front ends that hang down to the abdomen.

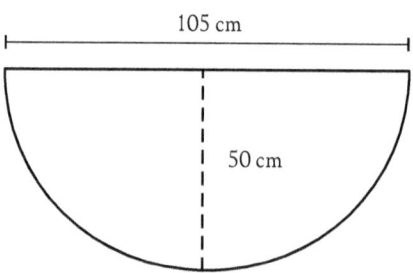

SEMICIRCULAR, SMALL
(the lower edge falls slightly above the shoulders)

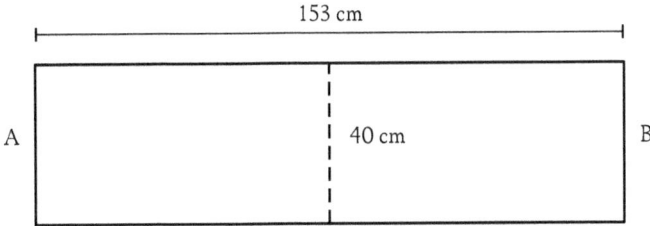

RECTANGULAR

This mantilla resembles common scarves or shawls. Usually the ratio of its length to its width is 2:1, 3:1, or even 4:1.

INFINITY VEILS

Infinity veils, also known as loop veils, derive their basic form from a rectangular veil as pictured above. To make a loop, attach (sew) side A and side B together, forming a tube. The actual measurements may be adjusted as preferred.

Betende in einer venezianischen Kirche
Ludwig Passini (1832–1903)

CHAPTER 6

The Mantilla Alone
Is Not Enough

T HAS BEEN RE-peatedly said in this book that in modern times, the mantilla is a form of devotion to the Blessed Sacrament. Wearing the mantilla can indeed be the beginning of greater reverence and love for the veiled Lord.

However, we must remember that the mantilla is a means, not an end. The ultimate goal of every devotion is to lead people to true appreciation of the faith in the mystery of God's saving work through Jesus Christ. In particular, the mantilla leads the wearer into a deeper appreciation of the Eucharistic Mystery. This love ought to take root, flourish, and reign in all aspects of our body and soul.

Below are other things that need to be seriously considered and practiced by mantilla wearers. Of course, these are all very good practices for anyone. But it is to be expected that a veiling woman will be "judged" more seriously because she has chosen to wear the garment that signifies the bride of Christ, and therefore she has all the more responsibility to act like one. Do not lose heart, sisters, because it is an honorable thing to examine your hearts and make them more conducive to receiving the grace of God and conforming yourselves more to His Will.

These fifteen points do not need to be practiced altogether spontaneously or simultaneously — it could become confusing and tiring, and perhaps also discouraging. Spiritual development is much like physical exercise for an athlete: both have to be built up gradually and the "difficulty level" must be increased only when ready. One also needs to remember that the time taken to progress in the spiritual journey is different for each person. So, start from the one closest to the practice of veiling, that is, the selection of clothes for Mass, and then continue to other points according to your ability.

GOING TO MASS

1. *What should I wear?* Even from the perspective of fashion alone, the beautiful lacy mantilla is a bad match for clothing that is too casual, too gaudy, too revealing, or too tight. Try to be more intentional about what kind of clothing is appropriate for you to wear to Holy Mass. Consider wearing a modest flare skirt that falls below the knees. The combination of a modest skirt or dress and a mantilla would certainly accentuate the feminine symbolism.

Indeed, choosing clothes for Mass should be a little inconvenient. If we are willing to be happily indecisive about what to wear to human parties, why are we not willing to give more thought to what we wear to our own wedding feast with Christ?

2. *Set your time well, and maintain silence.* As much as possible do not rush and do not be late to Mass. Allocate enough time so that you can still pray in

the church before the Mass begins. When you arrive at the church, maintain silence because now you are in the House of God. "Be still and know that I am God!" (Ps 46:11)

DURING THE MASS

3. *Give proper respect to the King.* If you have always paid respect to the Real Presence by genuflecting and making the sign of the cross, now do them with greater gravity! Do not make the sign of the cross as if shooing flies. Genuflect slowly, then — while still in the same position — bow your head in a moment of silence, then look up at the tabernacle and make the sign of the cross slowly and deliberately. Then rise up again and walk to your seat. Realize Who exactly you give your respect to, so that other people who happen to see you doing it would realize it too.

4. *The mind that seeks.* During the Mass, try to focus more and to participate actively. Active participation does not mean to sing loudly and speak all the time; it also includes active *internal* participation, or "active silence." So, when there comes a moment when the congregation is expected to be silent (for example, when the readings are proclaimed, when the priest is delivering his homily, or during the Eucharistic Prayer), use that moment as an opportunity for reflection or contemplation of the Great Mystery that is about to happen. Let your reason take part in the Mass!

5. *The eyes that worship.* When the priest elevates the host and then the chalice at consecration, look at them (do not look down!). And in your heart say the words of the Apostle Thomas, "My Lord and my God!" (*Dominus meus et Deus meus!*). As the host and

the chalice are brought down again, bow your head in deep reverence.

6. *The hands that pray.* Build a more intense prayer atmosphere with your hands! Train yourself during Mass—especially the part where the congregation stands (yes, including the Our Father, because the *orans* position is assumed only by the priest, not by the congregation)—to fold your hands together in front of your chest, palm to palm, as displayed by the altar servers. Of course, this can only be done if you are not holding a book or a piece of paper. But often we are already familiar with the songs, or there are no books or papers available, and our hands become "idle." When hands become "lazy," the result is postures or movements that are not very fitting for prayer. So, whenever you have the opportunity, fold your hands so that they actively worship Him too! Offer up the little inconvenience as a form of penance.

7. *The mouth that receives.* Do you receive Communion on the hand? Although this is allowed, remember that the norm is receiving Communion on the tongue, either while standing or kneeling. The mantilla is a symbol of humility and obedience; receiving Communion on the tongue—especially while kneeling—provides a more complete picture of receptivity and submission to God who feeds the Church, like a mother bird feeding her children who receive with open beaks. As long as you have healthy legs, use them to fall down in worship!

8. *The Lord still misses you.* After Mass, do not rush out! Make time for the One who made time itself as a gift. Give yourself more time to privately converse with Him who has created time for you.

AROUND THE MASS

9. *Increase the frequency of confession.* How often do you go to confession? Is it only twice, namely before Christmas and Easter? Increase it! Practice doing the examination of conscience every night before bed, and see how often you are in need of the Sacrament!

Increase the frequency of confession little by little, for example, get used to confessing every 6 months, then every 3 months, then every month. Throw away the mindset that the Sacrament of Penance is only for confessing mortal sins. Pope Pius XII in his encyclical *Mystici Corporis Christi* lists the other fruits of the Sacrament:

1. Genuine self-knowledge is increased;
2. Christian humility grows;
3. Bad habits are corrected;
4. Spiritual neglect and tepidity are resisted;
5. The conscience is purified;
6. The will is strengthened;
7. Salutary self-control is attained;
8. Grace is increased.

Go to confession often, even confessing venial sins. Nothing is more delightful to the Lord than His beloved receiving His Body with a clean soul.

10. *Improve the quality and frequency of Communion.* A very pious priest once told me, "One way to improve the *quality* of Communion is to increase its *quantity*!" If there is a church near you that celebrates Mass daily, make use of it. If it still feels difficult, try starting, for example, with First Fridays, then slowly increase to daily Mass. Accompany it with increasing the frequency of confession.

11. *Adoration and Visits.* If your church has an adoration chapel, go to Adoration as often as possible. If there is no adoration chapel, make a visit to the Blessed Sacrament kept in the tabernacle. Pray for a few minutes inside the church before the tabernacle. Take advantage of these intimate times together with your Lover. Do not forget the mantilla!

> Go to the encounter with him in the Blessed Eucharist, go to adore him in the churches, kneeling before the Tabernacle: Jesus will fill you with his love and will reveal to you the thoughts of his Heart. If you listen to him, you will feel ever more deeply the joy of belonging to his Mystical Body, the Church, which is the family of his disciples held close by the bond of unity and love.[1]

12. *Practice spiritual Communion.* Restore your genuine longing for Holy Communion by practicing spiritual Communion. Spiritual Communion may be done as often as desired, both outside and during the Mass (for example, if one is aware of a mortal sin that prevents one from receiving physical Communion). It is very easy: simply say a short prayer such as, "Jesus, I believe that Thou art really present in the tabernacle, in Thy Body, Blood, Soul and Divinity. Right now I cannot receive Thee sacramentally, but I ask Thee to come spiritually into my heart." Then let your heart rejoice and praise Him.

The practice of spiritual Communion is recommended by Pope Benedict XVI (*Sacramentum Caritatis,*

---

[1] Pope Benedict XVI, *Message to the Young Catholics of the Netherlands,* November 21, 2005.

55) and John Paul II (*Ecclesia de Eucharistia*, 34); see the classic texts by St. Thomas Aquinas (*Summa theologiae* III, Q. 80, arts. 1 and 2) and St. Teresa of Avila (*Way of Perfection*, chapter 35).

FROM THE MASS

13. *Learn and practice proper liturgy.* The mantilla may also be called a liturgical devotion, which means it is closely related to the worship of God through the Sacred Liturgy. A woman's obedience expressed in wearing the mantilla is the same obedience that ought to be expressed by the whole congregation to the Church's teachings, in this case regarding the order of the liturgy. If we obey our Heavenly Father, should we not also obey our Mother Church?

It is unfortunate to see liturgical abuses these days, either due to ignorance or due to pride and obstinacy. Instead of being like a child who, with a pure heart, receives a gift from his mother and gives thanks by using the gift well, a lot of people today look for "weak spots" in the order of the liturgy and fill them with creativity as much as possible, dangerously presuming on the Lord's mercy and tolerance.

Lay people do not have to wait for their priests to be the ones who correct liturgical abuses. The Congregation (now Dicastery) of Divine Worship and the Discipline of the Sacraments asserts that guarding the utmost dignity of the Most Holy Eucharist is everyone's responsibility.

> In an altogether particular manner, let everyone do all that is in their power to ensure that the Most Holy Sacrament of the Eucharist will be protected from any and every irreverence or distortion and that

> all abuses be thoroughly corrected. This is
> a most serious duty incumbent upon each
> and every one, and all are bound to carry
> it out without any favouritism.[2]

While the laity are often powerless to correct certain problems, they can always do what is within their power: kneel to receive Holy Communion; wear the veil; keep respectful silence before and after Mass; and respectfully make petitions to the local pastor and, if necessary, to the bishop. Therefore, start studying how the liturgy ought to be conducted, and observe it faithfully starting with yourself and then educating your closest ones. If you happen to be involved in liturgical matters, work hard to uphold and to guard the nobility of the Sacred Liturgy. Christian obedience has to be radical (i.e., from the roots up), including in the area of worship. At least, we women who wear the mantilla must neither *start* nor *support* any forms of liturgical abuse, because it is highly incongruent with the sign of obedience to Christ that we bear on our heads.

14. *Love the Church's other traditions.* The mantilla is only a tiny part of the abundant treasury of Church traditions. Do not let these traditions be forgotten like an unopened gift! What about the Latin language, the language of Church unity? Go learn it! What about Gregorian chants that used to caress the ears of the saints? Learn them as well! And what about traditional prayers and hymns? These beauties include the Angelus, Salve Regina, Prayer to St. Michael, Adoro Te Devote, Te Deum, and many

---

[2] Congregation for Divine Worship and the Discipline of the Sacraments, Instruction *Redemptionis Sacramentum*, no. 183.

others; they may be prayed privately or publicly, and they carry indulgences! Even if we have a hard time comprehending or memorizing them, that is not a reason to be discouraged—at the very least we must appreciate them and promote their use, and avoid hostility towards them.

15. *Ask for the grace of God.* All the above works have little worth without the oil of prayer. In your prayer, humbly ask for a special grace so that you and other Catholics may be able to love God in the Most Holy Eucharist even more. Pray also for priests, so that they remain faithful in their vocation, and become not only "good" priests but holy ones, who are truly aware of the dignity of priesthood and of the Great Mystery that they celebrate.

Reading
Joan Llimona (1860–1926)

CHAPTER 7

Each Veil Has a Tale

TESTIMONIALS ON
THE MANTILLA

HE FOLLOWING is a collection of testimonials generously contributed by Indonesian women from various parishes and dioceses in the country and abroad. Some already veil regularly, others have just started, still others are discerning. They have quite a handful of experiences to share with us. This collection also features testimonials from men, including two priests, who have witnessed women wearing mantillas. This shows that the noble simplicity displayed by wearing the mantilla is appreciated by men and is able to inspire them in a powerful way.

These writings have been minimally edited without changing the contents and by keeping the authentic writing style of each contributor. The English translation renders the Indonesian expressions as closely as possible.[1]

---

[1] These testimonials were gathered before the book's original publication in 2016. Because the age of each contributor at the

❊ ❊ ❊ ❊ ❊

In the city of Kupang, or in West Timor in general, the custom of wearing the mantilla has long been known as "the custom of East Timor." It could be due to the fact that under Portuguese influence, this tradition was never entirely abandoned by the people of East Timor (now the sovereign country of Timor Leste), even after the Second Vatican Council. The ladies, especially the older generation, veil themselves not only when they attend the Eucharistic celebration, but also when they go to confession, or when meeting a priest or the bishop for spiritual direction.

The Catholic Church, in the 1917 Code, Canon 1262, once obliged women to veil themselves, especially when they approached the sacred table. The Church used to require this, but the ruling has been abrogated, and even in Indonesia it is almost unknown. But lately, the mantilla is making a comeback everywhere in the world, including in Indonesia, especially among the Indonesian youth. This accompanies the increase of the celebration of the Traditional Latin Mass.

For me personally, the chapel veil or the mantilla is a symbol of holiness. In the liturgical context, the mantilla is a sign of a woman's purity, modesty, and humility, and also her obedience and glorification of God. The mantilla is one of the most specifically

---

time is relevant, the information has been left as-is. Similarly, at that time it was still common to speak of "Ordinary Form" and "Extraordinary Form." This terminology from *Summorum Pontificum* has been retired as of 2021, but it has been allowed to remain here.

feminine devotions. And because of this very nature, it is better to wear it all the time during liturgical celebrations. With the return of this beautiful practice, a woman is free to once again veil herself, as long as she's not doing it as a part of fashion trend, but rather with a true realization that the mantilla is a means to become closer to Our Lord Jesus Christ.

RD Patricius Neonnub
Diocesan priest of the Archdiocese of Kupang
Lecturer at St. Michael's Major Seminary[2], Kupang
Head of Catechetical Commission of
the Archdiocese of Kupang

---

[2] In Indonesian dioceses, Catholic seminaries are divided into two levels, minor and major. The *Seminari Menengah* (minor seminary) is a secondary-level seminary that accepts junior high school graduates (age 14–15). The duration of *Seminari Menengah* is usually three to four years, depending on the diocesan policy. Some dioceses offer a special section within *Seminari Menengah* called *Kelas Persiapan Atas (KPA)* or "Higher Preparation Section." This section is designed to prepare individuals who have already finished senior high school, are college students, or even young professionals, for entry into the *Seminari Tinggi* (major seminary).

While attending a minor seminary is not mandatory for entering a major seminary, some dioceses may require certain candidates to go through the KPA before they can enter the major seminary. The *Seminari Tinggi* (major seminary) begins with a *Tahun Orientasi Rohani* (TOR) or Spiritual Orientation Year. The purpose of TOR is to help seminarians develop the prayer life and spirituality of diocesan priests. After TOR, seminarians continue their formation through the study of philosophy and theology, which generally takes four to six years, depending on diocesan needs and policies. Before ordination to the diaconate, some dioceses may also include additional programs, such as pastoral years, where seminarians gain practical experience in the life and mission of the diocese.

░ ░ ░ ░ ░ ░

"What was sacred for prior generations, remains sacred and great for us as well, and cannot be suddenly prohibited altogether or even judged harmful" (Benedict XVI, Letter to the Bishops on the Occasion of the Publication of the Apostolic Letter "Motu Proprio Data" *Summorum Pontificum*).

The above quotation is what came to mind when I was asked to give some comments on the mantilla. For many Catholics, the mantilla, just like many other holy things of ages past, has become obsolete, an ancient relic irrelevant in modern times — and even in the extreme, forbidden, because it is deemed unsuitable to the "spirit of Vatican II."

In reality, no one conciliar document or post-conciliar liturgical document ever forbade the use of the mantilla. On the contrary, the mantilla may even support the growth of the sacred atmosphere because it symbolizes reverence before the Great King truly present in the small Host.

Sure, there is a saying, "*cucullus non facit monachum*" (the hood doesn't make the monk). It's true that piety must not stop at physical actions, at a prayer veil that drapes on the wearer's head. But as long as a human being still dwells in flesh and bone, he will always need physical instruments to help lift up his mind and his heart towards the celebrated Mystery. While wearing the mantilla, a woman lifts up her heart: "*habemus ad Dominum.*"

Our Holy Father Pope Benedict XVI points out that the two forms of the Latin Rite must enrich one another. Likewise, the wearing of the mantilla even in the Ordinary Form will aid our appreciation of the worship service. Let us then guard and again accustom ourselves to the use of the mantilla, one of the treasures of tradition of the Holy Church, as an expression of reverence to the Eucharist.

Benedictus Luki Anggoro Giri (31)
Master of Liturgical Ceremony of the
Apostolic Nunciature in Indonesia

✦ ✦ ✦ ✦ ✦

I started wearing the mantilla three months ago, more or less. There was this lady, a member of the parish's congregation, who was selling mantillas at the churchyard. I asked her, "What are these for?" She said, "These are chapel veils, they are called mantillas. Many women in Java already wear them." So I bought one, but I just kept it in my wardrobe, unused, for six months.

Then I came to think, why did I buy it if I never intended to use it? I tried googling everything I could about the mantilla. I discovered that veiling is an old tradition of the Church that is supported by a biblical passage that struck my heart (1 Cor 11:4 and 13). So I went on to wear it. It did feel odd at first. I was the only one veiling. I was nervous when I stood up to receive Communion because a lot of people were staring at me. A friend told me that some people even scrutinized me from top to bottom. But I strengthened my own heart, because I knew that this is the right thing to do and what ought to be.

Don't know if this is a coincidence or not, but since wearing the mantilla, I'm able to give myself more completely to prayer, even until I shed tears during the Holy Mass, out of the realisation that I am a sinner. Maybe this sounds a bit too much, but it's real; I realize that now I can be more attentive to the presence of the Lord.

My auntie is the closest person to me; she never said anything about my mantilla, but later I found out that she had secretly bought three mantillas! Some of my friends tease me. Most never say anything, although a few have expressed a desire to wear it too, but they don't have the courage just yet. The priests in my parish and in other parishes respond positively, though some also make friendly jokes about it, maybe because I look different.

My message is this: the mantilla is not a requirement, but it's better to wear it. Maybe we're afraid of being called "holier-than-thou," but don't we live this life on earth in order to strive to perfection? We run the race to become a better person, so if we know that this tradition is good and is even supported by the Scriptures, why don't we practice it? If you're afraid of people staring at you, well, it's only for the first few weeks. They'll get used to it, and perhaps more people will follow along. So, go wear the mantilla!

Maria Ostradella (22)
St. Mary Queen of the Rosary, Seberang Ulu, Palembang
Archdiocese of Palembang

※ ※ ※ ※ ※

Catholics wearing veils? What are they doing?? At first I didn't know that the chapel veil had been used way before I was born … The first time I received my veil, I thought, wow this would be so cool, this would make me feel like a nun or a bride … Then one night during a private prayer I tried the veil on, and wow, did I feel His presence immediately in front of me! My prayers felt more intimate, purposeful, and serious, be it private prayers or Mass with my community.

Irene Rosalina (26)
Redemptor Mundi, Surabaya
Diocese of Surabaya

❋ ❋ ❋ ❋ ❋

I started wearing the mantilla four months ago. I literally wept! Full of love, and it is as if the word "humility" flows over me! I think this chapel veil really did bring some positive changes in my spiritual life. Veiling at Mass is a way of living my vocation as a woman.

No one in my family is Catholic. They point out how every day I'm getting more and more freaky. Meanwhile, my best friend supports me and encourages me; she always says, don't be embarrassed and don't feel weird when people see you and compare you with others. The folks in my parish never really say anything... mostly they just stare at me. Once a woman sat beside me and she asked why I wore the veil, and where I bought it. She asked something that struck my heart: "Do you wear it to become like Mother Mary?"

My message for fellow ladies who are considering the mantilla is this: research as much as you can about this tradition, then ask yourself why you want to do it. Then, try the mantilla, and listen to your heart.

Audrey Susanto (29)
St. Luke the Evangelist, Sunter
Archdiocese of Jakarta

❋ ❋ ❋ ❋ ❋

In this secular age where people start forgetting and even ignoring their faith, culture, and manners, the presence of women wearing the mantilla during Holy Mass keeps my optimism for the future of the Church. Apparently there are still Catholics who faithfully prepare their body and soul for Mass because they understand Who they will receive in the Eucharist, that is, Lord Jesus the Bridegroom. Of course it's best when what is externally visible and what is contained interiorly are equally beautiful.

Greg (25)
Our Lady of the Assumption Cathedral of Jakarta
Archdiocese of Jakarta

❋ ❋ ❋ ❋ ❋

I've been wearing the mantilla for more than a year. My first mantilla was a gift from a Facebook friend. How amazing, after looking around for two years, I finally owned one! But I needed a few weeks until I actually wore it.

I braced myself to veil first to morning daily Mass, and then finally to Sunday Mass. I felt so peaceful. At last I could encounter Christ more modestly and more attentively. It wasn't very comfortable at first, of course, especially when I realized other people were whispering. But didn't I do it for the love of Christ? For the love of the Church's rich traditions? For the longing to see more people dress more appropriately at Mass? My hope is that those who whisper will find out about the mantilla and will love it too.

Wearing the mantilla doesn't mean we are better than others. Exactly because we're not holy, we need it to help us become better people. The mantilla has brought some positive changes in my spiritual life. I started to attend Mass more regularly with better interior preparation. I also participated more in Church activities, and was more motivated to pray and worship the Blessed Sacrament.

The priests, friars, and nuns in my parish are mostly supportive, although some do question it and even reject it. Indeed there are challenges in veiling. But one thing to remember is that the mantilla makes us realize that we are His humble servants. To be faithful is hard, but believe that it will yield sweet fruits. May I, too, remain faithful to Him who loves me first.

Mardianti Tandiarrang (26)
Immaculate Heart of the Blessed Virgin Mary, Makale
Archdiocese of Makassar

※ ※ ※ ※ ※

I'm in the process of preparing myself to veil. Hopefully soon I can commit myself to this devotion. I told my parents and they were supportive as long as I stay true to my conviction. Some other people though, especially my friends, they say, "But the Lord doesn't look at our appearance! Why do you want to follow that trend?" But fortunately, there are still many who encourage me.

Maria Yuliana Grace (22)
Beatae Mariae Virginis (BMV) Cathedral of Bogor
Diocese of Bogor

※ ※ ※ ※ ※

I wore the mantilla for the first time to an EF Mass at the chapel of Vincentius Putra Orphanage. I had been having the desire to veil for a while but never got around to it until the Mass at Vincentius because they provided free mantillas. Currently I still wear the mantilla only to EF Mass and OF Mass in certain places such as at the Apostolic Nunciature. I haven't had the courage to wear it in my own parish church because no one else wears it.

My family is pretty neutral about it, because they're not Catholic anyway. It's too bad that too many of our brothers and sisters do not know about the mantilla. Once I attended Mass at the Nunciature with parish church friends. I suggested they wear a mantilla or a scarf, but they said they'd never heard of this practice. So unfortunate.

To my sisters in faith, if you feel the call to wear a head covering at Mass, don't run from it! If you don't have the confidence to wear it to your parish church, wear it to EF Masses or Latin-language OF Masses. Together we learn to stand before the altar of the Lord in a more appropriate manner. If we don't start, then who will?

Yohana (26)
St. Paschal, Cempaka Putih
Archdiocese of Jakarta

※ ※ ※ ※ ※

I first wore the mantilla on February 2, 2014. Lots of people, including my own friends, stared at me weirdly. At first I felt really uncomfortable because I became the center of attention. A few days later, a friend told me that someone was wondering whether I've become a Muslim, but if so, why did I still attend the Holy Mass? My mum and dad, who usually sat beside me, started to leave me sitting by myself. I

was a little sad, but at least the priests never denied
me Holy Communion!

When I try to understand the mantilla as a sign
of obedience, I tell myself that if the local ordinary
wants me to leave aside the veil temporarily or for
ever, I will obey. But I pray to God that never happens! When I understand the mantilla as a sign of
chastity, it makes me become more aware of my
attire during Mass. It'd be odd if I cover my head
but flaunt the rest of my body, right?

True, wearing the mantilla doesn't automatically
make my life holy. But it gives me a kind of warning, that whatever looks good on the outside means
nothing if the inside is full of garbage — I mean sin.
In short, the biggest effect of wearing the mantilla for
me is a greater sensitivity towards sin. It makes me
want to attend the Holy Mass not only with proper
clothing but also with a better disposition. How do
I do it? It's simple! Go to confession regularly!

Terezia (33)
Good Shepherd, Pontianak
Archdiocese of Pontianak

▨ ▨ ▨ ▨ ▨

The first time I saw a woman wearing the chapel veil
was when I attended Mass in another parish church.
I was then amazed and perplexed... oh wow, there
is a devotion like that... I never knew!

Since I was a member of the parochial liturgy
team, I went on to research everything about the
mantilla. I discovered that veiling indeed has scrip-
tural and canonical foundations! I thought, "Why
don't we see this tradition anymore in my parish..."

After watching the movie *Les Miserables* and some

pictures of Korean ladies in mantilla, I became pretty impressed, "They look so sweet!" Well, for ladies who are still hesitant in wearing the mantilla, don't worry about starting it, because you have the bonus of looking cuter!

Paulus Jati Nugroho (33)
Calvary, Lubang Buaya
Archdiocese of Jakarta

▨ ▨ ▨ ▨ ▨

I've been veiling for two years. I don't only veil at EF Masses but also at Novus Ordo Masses. I veiled even before I knew about the EF Mass. I knew about this tradition from my close friend. The chapel veil has brought positive things for me. The veil is a kind of reminder for me to pray more personal prayers (before this I was a "Mass-only" person). The veil also reminds me to live more modestly (when veiling, we don't wear vulgar clothes) and more humbly (we are not holier than those who don't veil). The first time I veiled, I had to face both positive and negative comments from other people. I realized that I had to order my heart so that I don't fall into spiritual pride. For those considering the veil, when you're ready, it means you're ready to change into a new, better person.

M. M. Agustha Mandasari (29)
Redemptor Mundi, Surabaya
Diocese of Surabaya

▨ ▨ ▨ ▨ ▨

The first time I saw the chapel veil was in Korean dramas; there were scenes showing women wearing white and black veils. I thought it was only acting.

The second time was when I attended Mass in a parish in Java; I saw an elderly lady so deep in prayer while wearing the veil. I thought it was a Javanese or Malay tradition. But I was inspired to search for more information about it, and it turns out that the veil is really a Catholic tradition.

Some friends from the Social Commission [of the Archdiocese of Palembang] also veil at Mass. The congregation often gives them weird looks. Some time ago I saw a stranger who, when the church bell rang, quickly slipped a mantilla over her head. Again, people reacted weirdly. I thought, too bad a lot of people still don't know, or don't want to know, about this tradition.

Personally I think a woman in a mantilla looks so humble yet so graceful before the Lord. Of course I'd support it if this Catholic tradition is reintroduced in modern times. Let us go to the Lord with modesty and humility of heart.

Ch. Febrian Pratama S. (21)
Sacred Heart, Palembang
Archdiocese of Palembang

░ ░ ░ ░ ░

The mantilla is unique, I'd never seen it before. I mean, I'd never seen it in Indonesia, but I'm familiar with it thanks to TV documentaries about the Vatican. I just recently found out about its use in the country. It's pretty amazing. I do feel the urge to wear it, but I think I'm not yet accustomed to the traditional way. Of course, I'll give it some time, who knows if I will really wear it in the future. I think the mantilla is like adorning yourself for Him, from Whom our lives originate. I think it's very suitable for women to wear it to the Holy Mass because we are visiting His house. I also never consider those wearing it as "holier-than-thou," because I never judge people from their appearance.

Palinka (22)
St. Odilia, Citra Raya Cikupa
Archdiocese of Jakarta

❈ ❈ ❈ ❈ ❈

I've known the tradition of veiling at Mass since junior-high school, from the internet. I was stunned at how graceful the ladies looked in chapel veils. But more than that, I admired the radical intensity of their prayers when their heads were wrapped in mantillas. For me, the mantilla is a wonderful instrument from God specially for women to live out the mystery of faith radically, and also a sign of humility and obedience to Christ the Bridegroom. Moreover, as a guy, I feel that the chapel veil accentuates the true beauty of the woman wearing it. Thankfully, the Lord has moved my auntie to wear the mantilla. She once expressed her indescribable joy; she said she now could give herself totally into the Mystery of the Cross of Christ. In my own parish I think no woman practices this devotion yet. I really hope more women are called to veil at Mass and live out their calling as Christ's faithful brides.

Benediktus Diptyarsa Janardana (20)
St. Albert de Trapani, Blimbing
Diocese of Malang

❈ ❈ ❈ ❈ ❈

I've been veiling since 2008, not long after I came home to the Church (I was away for some twenty five years). The decision came after a long consideration as I was looking back on my way of life and the realization that I was "obsessed" with worldly things, among which was my hair and my looks. Around this time, I was also reading more about the more traditional church practice, of which veiling during Mass was a part. As the head covering for me was an attempt not to be so concerned with physical beauty, it also worked as a way for me to express my wish to return to tradition.

Every time I enter a church/chapel where the Blessed Sacrament is kept, I wear some form of head covering, whether it is for Mass or Adoration/Holy Hour or simply for my volunteer work as a chapel cleaner at a nearby convent. As long as I am in the same room where the Blessed Sacrament is kept, whether exposed or reposed, I wear some form of head covering. For work at the chapel, I wear a short headscarf, tied at the back, which is my standard daily head covering. For Mass and Adoration, I wear a shoulder wrap. I am able to be more focused during Mass as the veil limits my peripheral vision. During prayer outside of Mass, the head covering gives me a sense of warmth and safety, and it aids greatly in meditation.

The decision to veil must not come because one wants a certain look ("I want to look pretty by wearing a lacy hair accessory") or to be associated with a certain group ("I am more orthodox, I know more than most"). It must come from the desire to be more focused on praying by being less distracted by others (latecomers, chatty Mass goers, wearers of revealing clothes, etc.). But I think there is also the issue of charity. We are strongly advised to wear proper attire when attending Mass so as to be less of a distraction to others. Veiling can help. I myself have found it difficult to look away from glorious-looking hair within my line of sight during Mass; imagine how much more difficult it is for men. Thus, the charitable thing for a woman to do during Mass is to cover that glorious crown so that it will help others stay focused on God and not on worldly beauty.

Tiwi S. Wood (50)
St. Anthony of Padua, Fresno
Diocese of Fresno, California, USA

▩ ▩ ▩ ▩ ▩

The mantilla has been around for some long centuries. This head covering is a custom with a deep spiritual meaning. Since a woman's hair is her crown, when she's standing before the King of kings, it is better if she veils her crown.

Jeff (27)
St. Martin, Margahayu
Diocese of Bandung

▩ ▩ ▩ ▩ ▩

The mantilla is so attractive! In February 2015, I tried making my own mantilla from *tile* fabric and some lace. It was semicircular in shape. Boldly I wore it for the first time to the Holy Mass in St. Stanislaus, Girisonta. People around me were like, "Oh you look like a nun!" I just smiled. Some little kids asked me, "Sister, why are you wearing a *batik* dress?"

Now I veil regularly to Mass in my own parish church. Close friends and family never really said anything. Meanwhile, the other folks in my parish have varied comments. When I walked in line to receive Communion, some people yelled, "*Bu hajjah, bu hajjah!*"[3] Some others said I was trying to look cute, trying to be different, and so on. It's not a big deal, I simply accept it all. So far I'm the only woman with the mantilla in my parish; I feel confident and I'm trying to be faithful to the devotion.

With the mantilla, there's peace and consolation in my heart. I even started choosing more proper clothes to be worn to the house of the Lord. Don't wait until you're holy to wear the mantilla! I'm not holy myself, but I desire to be more humble before the Lord, and to glorify Him with my heart. Our external appearance is a reflection of our interior life, is it not?

Paulina Indra Haryati (37)
St. Paul Miki, Salatiga
Archdiocese of Semarang

❈ ❈ ❈ ❈ ❈

Personally, I like it when I see women veil at Mass and of course I'll be so happy if all women wear mantillas! I think veiling at Mass makes a woman look more modest, more proper, and more graceful. Besides, it adds more solemnity to the overall experience of the Mass.

I'm so impressed that lots of women in the Eastern Church veil themselves. How wonderful it would be if this practice were rejuvenated in the Roman Church.

---

3 In Indonesia, *hajjah* is an honorary title for a Muslim woman who has completed the hajj pilgrimage to Mecca; the male equivalent is *haji*. In other countries, these are not normally used as titles, so it is uncertain whether correct Anglicised versions of these titles exist. *Bu*, short for *Ibu*, means "Madam."

Doesn't Mother Mary veil herself too? I support the use of the mantilla but I would never force a woman to wear it. It all depends on how aware she is of the importance of modesty and humility.

Alvin Prima (24)
St. Alphonse Rodriguez, Pademangan
Archdiocese of Jakarta

朤 朤 朤 朤 朤

I began to be attracted to the chapel veil ever since I attended the baptism of my friend's baby in an Eastern Catholic Rite. Then I got interested in making my own mantilla with a more modern design. The Lord opened the way: my friend called me to buy my veil, and so she became my first client.

The first time I wore the mantilla to an English Mass at St. Theresia's Church, I felt a bit nervous because I was the only one veiling. But this feeling gradually disappeared during the Mass. When in my mantilla, I felt I became more attentive to the Holy Mass.

It turns out that a few friends also like it and have started wearing it, only on different occasions: some to Adoration, some in private prayers, some others when praying in a Marian shrine. I really suggest every woman wear the mantilla because you will be reminded of your own sanctity as a woman in the eyes of the Lord, and you will be motivated to imitate the faith and the humility of Our Lady.

Rita (37)
St. Christopher, Grogol
Archdiocese of Jakarta

朤 朤 朤 朤 朤

I started wearing the veil in Lent 2014. At first I was worried about being called a freak because no one else wore it. During the first few months, I only veiled when I wasn't singing in the choir, but when I had to be the conductor or a cantor, I would take it off for the sake of looking in uniform with the others. Some time later, another friend started wearing the mantilla, so now I have company! I'm now courageous enough to wear it when I'm singing in the liturgy.

There have been some changes in myself. I've become even more careful in selecting clothes to be worn to church. It's impossible to wear a chapel veil with a sexy dress! With veiling, I also became more aware of my own behaviors. It's not seemly if I veil myself but I'm busy chatting during Mass, or praying or singing with a bad attitude.

By wearing the chapel veil, it's like I'm inviting myself to behave better. Though some people look at me weirdly, my husband is supportive of it. My friends call me a freak, and a priest even made some sarcastic comments once. But others became curious and they started taking up the chapel veils too. One by one, priests gave us their approval.

Now I have several friends with chapel veils. Though I don't expect much, I hope in the future that people will at least be moved to wear more proper attire to church. With the resurgence of the chapel veil, I hope it will become an opportunity for reflecting on the modesty of our clothes.

Emmelia (35)
St. Peter, Lubuk Baja, Batam
Diocese of Pangkalpinang

※ ※ ※ ※ ※

I saw a chapel veil for the first time when I found
a First Communion photo of my auntie years ago. I
didn't know that it wasn't just an accessory. Slowly I
realized that the chapel veil is part of a long tradition
of the Catholic Church. Among my own relatives, I've
seen those who love Church traditions and teachings
also wear the chapel veil. In my parish there was this
lady who used to wear it, although she never does
anymore. Actually it would be really good if this practice is reintroduced, and I hope this tradition doesn't
remain a seasonal trend only. I hope people will
understand the deep meaning behind the chapel veil.

Gregorius Aditya (22)
Holy Cross, Tropodo
Diocese of Surabaya

※ ※ ※ ※ ※

I became familiar with the chapel veil in 2009 from
an online forum. In my own parish there's a lady who
always wears the mantilla to the Holy Mass. For me
personally, a woman will look more graceful when
she wears the chapel veil. It is also a way to imitate
Our Lady. She is always portrayed as a veiled woman,
so as her spiritual children, it's better if Catholic
women imitate their spiritual mother by veiling
during Mass and Adoration. I hope more Catholic
women will wear the chapel veil as an expression
of love, reverence, obedience, and humility before
Christ the Bridegroom.

Nicholas Adityas (19)
St. Robert Bellarmine, Cililitan
Archdiocese of Jakarta

❋ ❋ ❋ ❋ ❋

At first, the notion of Catholic women veiling sounded foreign to me. I wasn't aware that veiling had a special meaning and had been around since time immemorial. I thought it was only a local custom. But when I continued my study in the US, I came to see Christian women who veil themselves during prayer.

In the Roman Church, the typical veil I see is the lacy kind, called the mantilla. In the Eastern Church, especially in my parish, the veil is like a scarf wrapped around the head. I tried to find out why these women still veil themselves. Then I came across 1 Corinthians 11:1–16 and Canon 1262 from the older Code. So, apparently the head covering is no longer a requirement, but it is worn as a sign of reverence to God.

Actually I really like it when women veil during Mass, due to the spiritual meaning of the chapel veil. But since it is not a requirement, I'm pretty relaxed about it. My wife doesn't veil, so I'm fine with it. But most importantly, a woman's interior disposition and her clothing have to show reverence to the Lord.

Alwyn A. (31)
Holy Resurrection Melkite-Greek Catholic Church
Columbus, OH, USA

❋ ❋ ❋ ❋ ❋

At first, my reason to wear the lacy mantilla is because I liked the pretty design. So yeah, the initial motivation was really to look like a princess. But over time, the more I got to know the history of mantilla in the liturgy of the Catholic Church, and the more I read stories from women who decided to veil against all odds, and also through discernment and prayers, my motivation was purified and strengthened.

I no longer wear the mantilla just because it looks fancy and cute, but because of its religious meaning. I wear it because I feel the call to it. On October 5, 2014, on my 28th birthday, I braced myself to wear my first mantilla. I've worn it every time I go to church, whatever liturgy is celebrated (Eastern Catholic, Novus Ordo, or Traditional Latin Mass), and every time I go to Adoration.

When I stepped into my parish church in a black mantilla, I was feeling nervous because I was the only woman veiling. But anyway, after I went through it, it was fine...Some people did stare wonderingly, but not in a negative way. And I'm still confident about it, because when I look up at the large crucifix above the altar, I'm reminded again and again that I do this for Him.

Initially my family questioned my decision. But after I explained the meaning of the chapel veil and how I felt called to the devotion, they became okay with it. My church acquaintances, the nuns, and the priests who know me, complimented the decision. So it strengthened me even more. This experience is also a humbling one. In any case I wear the mantilla for Him because it is He who called me.

The mantilla reminds me to imitate Our Lady (who is also my patron saint), especially in humility, chastity, and obedience. I'm also reminded of the nature of my creation as a woman, as a "crown of creation," and of the dignity of woman as a precious treasure that needs to be veiled. Personally, the mantilla "forces" me to behave more appropriately wherever I am. Wearing the mantilla makes me able to focus more on the liturgy of the Holy Mass. I'm motivated to dress more modestly and more properly to Mass: my "Mass dress" is now a combination of a neat blouse, a modest midi-size skirt, shoes, and my black mantilla. I don't do this when going to church only; modest clothing has now become part of my lifestyle!

By wearing the mantilla, I want to invite other ladies to relive one of the Church's traditions, so beautiful, so wonderful, and so meaningful. For my fellow girls who secretly desire to wear the mantilla, discern and pray, and then wear it when your heart is ready. For guys whose girlfriends or wives long to wear the mantilla, please support them and pray for them, and please don't call them freaks!

Rosa Mystica (29)
Our Lady of Mount Carmel, Tomang
Archdiocese of Jakarta

▨ ▨ ▨ ▨ ▨

I first wore the chapel veil when I assisted at the TLM in Yogyakarta, in 2011. I routinely wear a mantilla in the TLM, whereas in the Ordinary Form I wear it only when I serve as a lector.

I have invited the other female members of my choir group to wear the mantilla, but they said they weren't ready yet. But they also said they would wear it next year when we'll go on a pilgrimage to the Marian shrine of Wonosobo, in order to respect the local church whose faithful are already accustomed to wearing the mantilla. My friends from the prayer group already started veiling but it's still limited to Masses in their own community.

Several priests expressed their support when I put up a picture of me in a mantilla as a Messenger display picture.

N. N. (43)
St. Joseph, Gedangan
Archdiocese of Semarang

▧ ▧ ▧ ▧ ▧

I've been wearing the mantilla for about ten months. Well, I do feel "different," and at first I was bit embarrassed too, actually. But there are some positive spiritual changes that are quite big . . . I'm now more passionate in celebrating the Holy Mass, and at the same time I feel more solemn, and humbled before the Lord. I'm also more excited to join other church activities. Some people say they admire the spirituality of veiling, but there are others who stare at me, and some also scoff at me. Most of them just stare, though. If someone asks, "Why do you veil in church?" I usually answer, "It's for modesty, like Mother Mary. This is an old Catholic tradition that has long been abandoned. I just want to try to return to it. The basic principle is outlined in 1 Corinthians 11."

For other girls who still hesitate to wear the mantilla, let me say this: we have to realize why we do this, and for whom. Don't we veil for Christ? So, no need to be embarrassed, our little effort in pleasing Him will be a bonus point in the eyes of the Lord.

Maria Megawati Heviputri (18)
Beatae Mariae Virginis Cathedral of Bogor
Diocese of Bogor

▧ ▧ ▧ ▧ ▧

Actually I've known about the mantilla since childhood, because it is my grandmother's culture; she was of Portuguese-Spanish descent. I remember, every time we were getting ready for church, our mantillas were prepared on the small prayer table, near the crucifix, the rosary, and the statues. Grandma would be very angry if we went to church without our mantillas on. So we've been accustomed to this practice even though other people saw us as oddities, and even though we did not know the term "mantilla." Grandma called it *hoofddoek*, a Dutch word that means a veil or a head covering.

Grandma used to sew her own mantillas that she gave to all her daughters and granddaughters. But this family tradition slowly faded when we were married, because Grandma couldn't monitor us anymore. Only recently when I browsed the internet and Facebook did I see that the tradition of veiling has begun to reappear. I remembered, "Oh, this is what Grandma used to wear!" and so I felt encouraged to start wearing it again. I haven't found a "real" mantilla, so I just use an ordinary scarf.

Because of this habit, people know me as "*Ibu hajjah*." Most of them only tease playfully, though there are a few who actually scorn me, but not a lot. I don't pay attention to it. It goes in one ear and out the other. They are now used to seeing me veiled anyway.

I never have any problems with priests about this. On the contrary, one priest I once asked regarding veiling, said that veiling in Mass is a good tradition, and we shouldn't be ashamed to practice it.

For me, the mantilla or chapel veil is not just a piece of clothing, but it has a meaning and it influences my spiritual life. I feel my prayers have become more focused. I feel that my spiritual development is going quite fast. I have also become more aware of the liturgy and its correct gestures.

For those who already wear the mantilla, that's great—please continue to do so! And for those who are still considering, don't hesitate and don't be afraid to preserve such a good tradition.

Elisabeth Mait (62)
Our Lady Flower of Carmel, Meruya
Archdiocese of Jakarta

▨ ▨ ▨ ▨ ▨

A veil that is worn by a woman during Mass is in fact not foreign to me. I've seen it ever since I was little. A lot of ladies back in my village wore veils to Mass. At Kampung Sawah, a suburb of Jakarta, again I saw veils being worn during Holy Mass.

At that time, though, I didn't know there was a connection between veiling and the Holy Mass. I simply thought it was the individual culture of the wearer. I didn't know the Church once ruled that women were obliged to cover their heads during Mass. Since the new Canon Law of 1983 was put into effect, the obligation no longer existed. I myself rediscovered the practice when I was requested to celebrate the Mass in the Extraordinary Form in Bandung, in the year 2013.

I now see women wearing chapel veils even outside the Extraordinary Form. In my parish there are two of them. This is a good thing. The chapel veil, called a "mantilla," is no longer required, but it can be a good instrument for learning to dress properly for Mass. I think a woman who veils herself at Mass looks like Our Lady. We see how almost all statues of Our Lady portray her modestly veiled. And indeed she used to veil during her earthly life. It is pretty straightforward: the mantilla is the garment of the Blessed Virgin. Maybe it sounds a bit too simplistic, but this simple way of thinking will help nurture and deepen our faith, especially our faith in the Eucharist.

RD Y. Istimoer Bayu Ajie
Diocesan priest of the Diocese of Bandung
Episcopal Master of Liturgical Ceremony
of the Diocese of Bandung

A Young Woman Outside a Church
Charles Louis Müller (1815–1892)

We Come to Worship Him

THE MANTILLA, REPENTANCE, AND KNEELING TO RECEIVE COMMUNION

Cornelius Pulung[1]

> [May I] receive the Bread of Angels, the King of kings, the Lord of lords, with that reverence and humility, with that contrition and devotion, with that purity and faith, with that resolve and intention which is expedient for the salvation of my soul.
>
> —St. Thomas Aquinas

EARING the chapel veil (mantilla) and receiving Communion on the tongue while kneeling: what are the similarities between the two? The answer is quite obvious: they may be said to have practically disappeared after the Second Vatican Council, and have become unknown to most of the faithful. This article is not

---

[1] Cornelius Pulung holds a Bachelor of Psychology from Universitas Katolik Atma Jaya, Jakarta, Indonesia.

meant to elaborate the reasons behind such disappearance. Nevertheless, in recent years, a number of Catholics have rediscovered these beautiful practices. This clearly cannot be separated from the role of Pope Benedict XVI who, through his Motu Proprio *Summorum Pontificum*, made it possible for the clergy and the faithful to again celebrate the Traditional Latin Mass. We all know that in the TLM, the ladies are expected to wear the chapel veil, and everyone is required to receive Communion on the tongue while kneeling.

Why is there a need to revive the practices of veiling and receiving Communion on the tongue while kneeling? Are they not uncommon, and no longer obligatory? Is this only a trend, or is there really something more, something deeper, that speaks to us and calls us to adopt them once again?

My personal experience shows how, at least in Indonesia, the two practices seem to lack support from the clergy. I know some friends who were not given Holy Communion, by a priest or by an extraordinary minister, because they wanted to receive on the tongue while kneeling. Another priest once reproved me because the way I receive Communion was thought to be "outdated" and "medieval." Why do we want to go back to the past, when the Church is always moving forward?

As for the mantilla, I too know a priest who explicitly shows his disapproval towards those wearing it. Moreover, mantilla-wearers are often scrutinized by the rest of the congregation, because the mantilla makes these ladies look odd. Some even say that it makes one look like a Muslim (and consequently less Catholic?).

Anyone who adopts these traditional practices only to follow a seasonal trend will surely be disillusioned when confronted with opposition or criticism. But those who are mature in their faith must be ready to hold themselves accountable for everything they do (cf. 1 Pt 3:15).

MANTILLA: A FIRST STEP TO CONVERSION

Sumunt boni, sumunt mali: Both the wicked and the good
sorte tamen inaequali,   eat of this celestial Food:
vitae vel interitus.   but with ends how opposite!
Mors est malis, vita bonis: Here it is life: there it is death:
vide paris sumptionis   the same, yet issuing to each
quam sit dispar exitus.   in a difference infinite.[2]

The mantilla must be understood in the Eucharistic context, because Catholic ladies veil themselves especially during the Holy Mass. No need to elaborate further on the meaning of the mantilla as a symbol of sanctity, purity, and reverence to God, as the author of this book has explained it well. One thing that merits the spotlight here is the connection between the mantilla and one's self-conversion, and its place in the context of the Eucharist.

Cardinal Ratzinger (Pope Benedict XVI) defines this conversion as follows:

> The Greek word for converting means: to rethink—to question one's own and common way of living; to allow God to enter into the criteria of one's life; to not merely judge according to the current opinions. Thereby, to convert means: not to live as all the others live, not do what all do, not

---

2 St. Thomas, *Lauda Sion Salvatorem.*

feel justified in dubious, ambiguous, evil actions just because others do the same; to begin to see one's life through the eyes of God; thereby looking for the good, even if uncomfortable; not aiming at the judgment of the majority, of men, but at the justice of God—in other words: to look for a new style of life, a new life.[3]

Receiving Communion on the tongue while kneeling has become uncommon, and so has wearing the mantilla. I (and perhaps you too) have never been taught about them by any religion teachers or priests. Consequently, the decision ultimately taken to practice them must first be preceded by a pursuit of truth, followed by a deep reflection that we do these things to please God only, and not to seek or even enjoy the praises of men, and not just to look different or physically attractive. The decision then ought to follow a thorough examination of conscience; in other words, wearing the mantilla for the first time must be the beginning of "not [living] as all the others live, not [doing] what all do," the beginning of "[seeing] one's life through the eyes of God; thereby looking for the good, even if uncomfortable." In short, the mantilla must be the first step towards a true conversion of self.

A true conversion is not only a matter of intellectual shift, but it demands a total transformation of our whole being. It is not enough to change our mindset and our behavior; conversion needs repentance—an actual sorrow for sin—not only in the

---

[3] Address to Catechists and Religion Teachers "On the New Evangelization," December 10, 2000.

heart but also expressed in the confession of one's sins. His Excellency Antonio Guido Filipazzi, the Apostolic Nuncio to Indonesia, pointed this out:

> It is not enough to do just an act of internal repentance, because true repentance implies always the intention to go to Confession. Also, we cannot turn directly to God to receive pardon, rejecting the way that God Himself has established for us to receive the forgiveness of sins. A medieval author reminds us that "Bridegroom and Bride, that is Christ and the Church, are as one, be it in receiving confession or in bestowing absolution... The Church is incapable of forgiving any sin without Christ, and Christ is unwilling to forgive any sin without the Church."[4]

We must always remember that those in the state of mortal sin may not receive the Eucharist: "For anyone who eats and drinks without discerning the body, eats and drinks judgment on himself" (1 Cor 11:29). St. Paul's warning ought to be heeded and followed, lest we commit sacrilege when we receive the Body of the Lord unworthily. Additionally, on preparing oneself before receiving the Eucharist, the Catechism of Trent teaches that "the great and exalted gifts of God, when received into a soul properly disposed, are of the greatest assistance towards the attainment of salvation; while to those who receive them unworthily, they bring with them eternal death."

---

[4] Homily at the Opening Mass of the Third Asian Apostolic Congress on Mercy, October 14, 2015, citing Isaac of Stella, *Sermon 11.*

Thus, before a woman takes up the mantilla, she ought to realize that the thing that needs experiential transformation, that is, conversion, is her heart, her internal disposition. The longing to love God, to praise and glorify Christ in the Eucharist, expressed in this case by the practice of veiling, always presupposes a true conversion. Wearing the mantilla, when accompanied by the effort to confess sins regularly, to continuously cleanse oneself in order to receive the Eucharist worthily, will become a good means for educating the faithful in reverence towards the Eucharist and enabling them to "see one's life through the eyes of God." If ladies take up this traditional practice freely and in full awareness of the spiritual responsibility, they will become real witnesses of the mercy of God found in the Sacrament of Penance, and they will also preach once again the truth of the Christian faith that the Eucharist is a sacrament for those reconciled to the Lord, not a mere meal of unrepentant sinners. The Eucharist, first and foremost, is a sacrament for converted sinners.

KNEELING BEFORE THE LORD

> Because of this, God greatly exalted him and bestowed on him the name that is above every name, that at the name of Jesus every knee should bend, of those in heaven and on earth and under the earth, and every tongue confess that Jesus Christ is Lord, to the glory of God the Father. (Phil 2:9-11)

"Kneeling does not come from any culture—it comes from the Bible and its knowledge of God."[5]

---

[5] Ratzinger, *The Spirit of the Liturgy*, 185.

Several biblical passages[6] from the New Testament portray kneeling as intimately associated with the recognition of God's divinity and man's unworthiness.

In the Gospel of Mark, a leper approached Jesus, and, kneeling down, begged for His help, saying: "If you wish, you can make me clean" (Mk 1:40). The Gospel of John tells us about a blind man healed by Jesus, yet the Pharisees did not believe the man's story.

> When Jesus heard that they had thrown him out, he found him and said, "Do you believe in the Son of Man?" He answered and said, "Who is he, sir, that I may believe in him?" Jesus said to him, "You have seen him and the one speaking with you is he." He said, "I do believe, Lord," and he worshiped him. (John 9:35–38)

We are no different from the leper and the blind man. Who are they to receive His healing, His miracles? And who are we that the same Lord is willing to descend to earth, to give Himself to us in the Holy Eucharist? In St. Thomas Aquinas's Prayer Before Communion, we are continually reminded of our unworthiness and poverty: "As one infirm, I approach the balm of life; as one begrimed, the fountain of mercy; as one blind, the light of eternal splendor; as one poor and needy, the Lord of heaven and earth."

The Eucharist reveals to us an eternal truth, "ever ancient, ever new" (St. Augustine). Pope Benedict XVI elegantly describes this beautiful and profound truth:

6 A more in-depth explanation on kneeling may be read in *The Spirit of the Liturgy* by Cardinal Ratzinger. In the chapter "The Body and the Liturgy," Ratzinger gives some relevant examples from both Old and New Testaments. This chapter may be accessed online at https://adoremus.org/2002/11/the-theology-of-kneeling/.

> We Christians kneel only before God or
> before the Most Blessed Sacrament because
> we know and believe that the one true
> God is present in it, the God who created
> the world and so loved it that he gave his
> Only Begotten Son (cf. Jn 3:16).... Ador-
> ing the Body of Christ means believing
> that there, in that piece of Bread, Christ
> is really there, and gives true sense to life,
> to the immense universe as to the smallest
> creature, to the whole of human history as
> to the most brief existence.[7]

Ratzinger speaks about the symbolism of kneeling in the Old Testament: it conveys giving one's
strength over to God.

> In the Hebrew of the Old Testament, the
> verb *barak*, "to kneel," is cognate with the
> word *berek*, "knee." The Hebrews regarded
> the knees as a symbol of strength; to bend
> the knee is, therefore, to bend our strength
> before the living God, an acknowledgment
> of the fact that all that we are we receive
> from Him.[8]

Kneeling is important because there is an inseparable
bond between its physical meaning and its spiritual
value, as Ratzinger goes on to say:

> The bodily gesture itself is the bearer of
> the spiritual meaning, which is precisely
> that of worship. Without the worship,
> the bodily gesture would be meaningless,
> while the spiritual act must of its very

---

[7] Homily on the Solemnity of Corpus Christi, May 22, 2008.
[8] *The Spirit of the Liturgy*, 191.

nature, because of the psychosomatic unity
of man, express itself in the bodily gesture.... When kneeling becomes merely
external, a merely physical act, it becomes
meaningless. On the other hand, when
someone tries to take worship back into
the purely spiritual realm and refuses to
give it embodied form, the act of worship
evaporates, for what is purely spiritual is
inappropriate to the nature of man. Worship is one of those fundamental acts that
affects the whole man. That is why bending
the knee before the presence of the living
God is something we cannot abandon.[9]

Kneeling during Communion is always accompanied by receiving on the tongue. Although one may
receive on the tongue while standing, receiving on
the tongue is theologically more compatible with the
gesture of kneeling. Receiving Communion on the
tongue shows great recognition that the Eucharist
is a gift, given not as a reward for man's merit, but
solely out of God's goodness and mercy. The gesture
of receiving the Sacred Host on the hand, picking it
up and putting it in one's mouth, still contains some
sort of autonomy or power on man's part, whereas
receiving it directly on the tongue shows total depen-
dence on God. Moreover, the specific set of motions
where one *picks* up the Host and *puts* it in his own
mouth reminds me of the story of the Fall of Man:
our First Parents disobeyed God's law by *picking* and
putting in their own mouths the fruit of the tree of
the knowledge of good and evil.

---

9 Ibid.

WE COME TO WORSHIP HIM

> The foolish [virgins], when taking their
> lamps, brought no oil with them, but
> the wise brought flasks of oil with their
> lamps.... The bridegroom came and those
> who were ready went into the wedding
> feast with him. Then the door was locked.
> Afterwards the other virgins came and said,
> "Lord, Lord, open the door for us!" But he
> said in reply, "Amen, I say to you, I do
> not know you." Therefore, stay awake, for
> you know neither the day nor the hour.
> (Mt 25:3-4, 10-13)

When I reflect on the bridal characteristic of the
mantilla, I immediately recall this particular proverb.
The wise virgins and the foolish virgins demonstrate
very different approaches in welcoming the bridegroom. The wise virgins have prepared both the lamps
and the oil, while the foolish ones bring only the
lamps without the oil.

The ten virgins may be interpreted in several ways:
they may symbolize the entirety of mankind, or the
whole Christian faithful, or, much more narrowly,
those who consecrate their virginity. The best inter-
pretation, however, is that they symbolize those who
possess the faith (and those lacking in it). The lamp
symbolizes faith, and the oil symbolizes charity that
makes faith alive and saving. Faith without charity
does not save. The locked door that makes the foolish
virgins unable to enter into the wedding feast is the
perdition that befalls one in mortal sin.

This proverb underscores the need to stay awake
spiritually, because we never know when Christ the
Bridegroom will come. This vigilance is maintained

by regular examination of conscience and confession, because only the clean and pure soul may enter eternal happiness, whereas those persisting in mortal sin even unto death will be cast into perpetual torment, that is, Hell. When a person dies, his soul immediately stands before the judgment of the Lord; if he has not prepared himself, he will earn the same fate that crushes the foolish virgins: "Amen, I say to you, I do not know you."

Yet there is a coming of the Bridegroom whose time we *can* know of, and that is during the Holy Mass. Likewise, this encounter with Christ in the Eucharist presupposes a preparation beforehand, that is, a state of grace, so that the most august Sacrament that we receive "will not condemn [us] to punishment but will rather secure [our] forgiveness."[10]

This internal disposition of the wise virgins is one that needs to be possessed by all the faithful, especially the ladies who wear the mantilla. We wait upon His coming, while staying vigilant and keeping watch of our souls, and always remembering to honor and worship the Lord with flaming love. Wearing the mantilla can be a reminder for ladies to stay on guard, for only those who keep watch are able to enter into the wedding feast of the Bridegroom.

The encounter and union with Christ in the Eucharist will be even more appropriate and beautiful when we respond with an act of adoration: by receiving Him on the tongue while kneeling. Once again, Ratzinger explains why: "The One whom we adore ... is not some distant power. He

---

[10] St. Thomas Aquinas, "Longer Prayer After Communion," in *The Aquinas Prayer Book*, 81.

has himself knelt down before us to wash our feet. And that gives to our adoration the quality of being unforced, adoration in joy and in hope, because we are bowing down before him who himself bowed down, because we bow down to enter into a love that does not make slaves of us but transforms us."[11] And again: "Eating [the Eucharist]...is a spiritual process, involving the whole man. 'Eating' it means worshiping it."[12] After a good preparation by means of the Sacrament of Reconciliation, it is right that we adopt the best gesture of worship, the one that best shows profound reverence, that stresses there is a Mystery most extraordinary and most noble; a gesture that witnesses that what we receive is no longer mere bread and mere wine, but the Body, Blood, Soul, and Divinity of the Most Holy Lord. This truth of the faith, I think, is only fully revealed when one receives on the tongue while kneeling. Although there is no obligation to do so, nor to do so while wearing a veil, both practices truly reflect the majesty of the Eucharist. Both are pleasing to God when done out of love for Him.

Wearing the mantilla and kneeling when receiving Communion on the tongue are harmonious with each other. They are not practiced because one feels nostalgic, or out of the desire of "wanting to go back to the past." They are practiced in order to preserve and propagate the perpetual truth of the faith; whatever is conducive to the reverence towards the Eucharist must be given a high priority in the life of the faithful. The Holy Eucharist received "with reverence and humility, with contrition and

---

11 Ratzinger, *God Is Near Us*, 113.
12 Ratzinger, *The Spirit of the Liturgy*, 90.

devotion, with purity and faith, with resolve and intention expedient for the salvation of the soul"[13] will enable the faithful to renew their love for God by proclaiming: "Truly, we come to worship Him!" Wearing the mantilla and receiving Communion on the tongue while kneeling, with the correct internal disposition, is a real act of worship. "So let us ask the Lord that he may grant us to understand this and to rejoice in it and that this understanding and this joy may spread out from this day far and wide into our country and our everyday life."[14]

---

[13] Cf. St. Thomas Aquinas, "Before Communion," in *Aquinas Prayer Book*, 75.
[14] Ratzinger, *God Is Near Us*, 113.

The Revival and Rediscovery of Head Coverings for Women

A CANONICAL POINT OF VIEW

A Dominican Friar

THE REQUIREMENT to wear a veil, or mantilla, or head covering for women is one of the many canons from the 1917 Code of Canon Law that were abrogated by the 1983 Code of Canon Law. It is said in Canon 1262 §2: "Women, however, shall have a covered head and be modestly dressed, especially when they approach the table of the Lord." We might be surprised to learn that many canons concerning liturgical discipline in the 1917 Code were re-ordered or abolished in the codification of the 1983 Code.

So, how can this noble canon regarding the head covering for women, which was tested through centuries and had a biblical basis, be abolished?

We tend to have a negative sense in understanding the terms "abrogation," "revocation," and "reordering."

We think that if something is abrogated, revoked, reordered, and abolished, it is because the former regulations or norms are no longer useful or essential for our present-day situation. With this understanding, we expect new regulations or norms to be introduced.

The abolishment of the canon regarding head covering for women might sadden us and bring unsolved questions to our minds. However, if we try to see the spirit behind the revision of the Code and the Second Vatican Council, we may instead find encouragement for the "revival" movement of veiling in our Church today.

BEHIND 1262 §2 OF THE 1917 CODE

The norms regarding head covering for women are part of the liturgical norms regulating "things" that encompass Canons 726–1551 of the 1917 Code. Here is the larger context of Canon 1262 of the 1917 Code:

Book I. [...]
Book II. [...]
Book III. Things (Cc. 726–1551)
  Part I. [...]
  Part II. [...]
  Part III. Divine Worship
    Section 1. General Principles (cc. 1255–1264)
      Decrees of Kinds of Worship (c. 1255)
      Public and Private Worship (c. 1256)
      Exclusive Authority of Holy See Over
        Liturgical Worship (c. 1257)
      Co-operation in Worship with Non-
        Catholics (c. 1258)
      Authority of the Ordinary (c. 1259)
      Ministers of Worship Subject to Ecclesiastical Authority (c. 1260)

The canon regulating head covering for women is
listed under Part III, Section 1: "Norms for Persons
Assisting at Worship." It is a disciplinary canon with
a rich biblical, historical, and theological background.
However, it does not mean that this ancient practice
is without any challenges. For example, in China, the
custom among men of keeping the head covered was
a sign of respect. So, the missionaries wrote a letter
to the Sacred Congregation for the Propagation of
the Faith to allow Chinese men to keep their heads
covered during liturgical celebrations.[1] The Sacred
Congregation responded positively to the proposal on
October 18, 1883. Thus, we see that the disposition of
the legislators of the 1917 Code when they codified
the rule for head covering is one of some flexibility,
depending on popular customs as long as permission
was granted by the Holy See.

A proof that Canon 1262 §2 of the 1917 Code was
deemed important is that the Holy See made use
of it in addressing modesty in women's dress. An
instruction containing twelve points on this matter
was issued by the Sacred Congregation of the Holy
Office (now the Dicastery for the Doctrine of Faith)
in 1930.[2] The instruction was signed by Cardinal

---

[1] S. C. Prop. Fid., 18 Oct. 1883; *Collectanea*, n. 1606, ad XVI.
[2] S. C. Conc., 12 Jan., 1930; *AAS*, 22–26; Digest, I, p. 212.

Donato Sbarretti, the Prefect of the Sacred Congregation, with the blessing of Pope Pius XI. The instruction tried to safeguard women's modesty in various ways, e.g., through preaching by priests, policies of Catholic schools, formation by Catholic parents, and so forth.

The Church's greater concern for women's modesty most probably came in the "flapper" era that took hold around the 1920s, just after World War I. The "flapper" era endorsed the figure of a "free," modern woman who rebelled against the stricter, more old-fashioned, Victorian ways. Commercially too, for the first time ever, women were being marketed to in high volumes, which boosted the sales of cosmetics and perfumes. The combining of several different elaborate fabrics for evening wear had become very popular. Dresses could be ornately decorated with glass beads, rhinestones, furs, and fabric flowers in a way that accentuated the body sensually, drawing the wrong sort of attention to it and detracting from attention given to the whole person. It was a gradual, yet profound, social and cultural shift. The instruction of the Sacred Congregation of Holy Office became a timely and serious reminder for the Church and the society to protect the dignity of women.

REVISION OF THE CODE

The revised codification follows the categories accepted by Vatican II, namely, the *munera*, of the offices of the Church: the teaching office (Book III), the sanctifying office (Book IV), and the rights and duties of rulers and subjects (Book II). This pattern of the revised Code confines Book IV to the ordering of the liturgical and sacramental life of the

Christian people. Book IV of the 1983 Code reflects a major simplification in the quantity as well as the substance of the canons. It reduces about 600 canons of the 1917 Code to a little more than 400![3] The regulation regarding head covering for women is one of the "victims" of this simplification in the 1983 Code of Canon Law.

First, let us consider two canons of the 1983 Code of Canon Law: Canon 2 and Canon 6.

Canon 2 states:

> For the most part the Code does not define the rites which must be observed in celebrating liturgical actions. Therefore, liturgical laws in force until now retain their force unless one of them is contrary to the canons of the Code.

This implies that there are canons that *do* regulate the liturgy, but we are to seek sources outside the Code of Canon Law itself. These other sources are the directories or instructions published by the Roman Curia on liturgical matters, rubrics, and the juridical norms in the introduction of the liturgical books.

Canon 6 is about the status of the previous law:

§1. When this code takes force, the following are abrogated:
    1° the Code of Canon Law promulgated in 1917;
    2° other universal or particular laws contrary to the prescripts of this Code unless other provision is expressly made for particular laws;

---

[3] John B. Beal, Thomas J. Green, et al., eds., *New Commentary on the Code of Canon Law* (Bengaluru: Theological Publication, 2019), 999.

      3° any universal or particular penal laws what-
soever issued by the Apostolic See unless
they are contained in this Code;

      4° other universal disciplinary laws regarding
matter which this code completely reorders.

§2. Insofar as they repeat the former law, the
canons of this Code must be assessed also in
accord with canonical tradition.

This canon intends to provide juridical certainty
regarding the relationship of the 1983 Code to the
1917 Code previously enacted.[4]

In light of Canon 6, the regulation regarding head
covering for women in Canon 1262 §2 of the 1917
Code of Canon Law is part of the abrogated material since it is not repeated or reformulated in the
1983 Code of Canon Law. The regulation regarding
head covering can be found nowhere in liturgical
norms after the Second Vatican Council. There is
no mention of the head covering for women in any
of the sources of liturgical norms after the Second
Vatican Council. Thus, head covering for women is
no longer required in every liturgical celebration in the
Church. Nevertheless, at the same time *the practice is
not prohibited by the Church*. In other words: it is entirely
permissible, and, we might even argue, praiseworthy.

ABROGATION OF CANON 1262 OF THE 1917
CODE: A BLESSING IN DISGUISE

We may wonder about the reason for the abrogation of Canon 1262 of the 1917 Code from the
revised Code and the general silence about this noble
liturgical practice after the Second Vatican Council.

---

4 Ibid., 54.

There is no formal explanation from the Pontifical Council of Legislative Texts regarding the removal of several canons of the 1917 Code one by one, unless we have access to the discussions of the Commission on the Revision of the Code that led to the decision.

Nevertheless, the answer might be found in the Second Vatican Council's Constitution on the Sacred Liturgy *Sacrosanctum Concilium*:

> Even in the liturgy, the Church has no wish to impose a rigid uniformity in matters which do not implicate the faith or the good of the whole community; rather does she respect and foster the genius and talents of the various races and peoples. Anything in these peoples' way of life which is not indissolubly bound up with superstition and error she studies with sympathy and, if possible, preserves intact. Sometimes in fact she admits such things into the liturgy itself, so long as they harmonize with its true and authentic spirit.[5]

One reason for removing Canon 1262 of the 1917 Code might be to avoid rigid uniformity in matters that do not implicate the faith. The Commission might have deemed that the regulation of the head covering for women was too rigid. This consideration is certainly unlike that of the canonical regulation on the matter and form of the Sacraments, which will affect their validity. Wearing a head covering might not *seem* necessary for the good of the whole community anymore, so the Church leaves it to the discretion of individuals.

---

[5] *Sacrosanctum Concilium*, art. 37.

Despite this abrogation, some parts of the world still continue the practice. Instead of looking at head covering as an outdated, "pre-Vatican II" practice, many of the faithful consider it a noble custom because of its importance in promoting modesty. Some regard the practice of covering the head during Mass, and even when entering a church, as part of their culture already. Some regard it as part of the "rediscovery" of the rich treasures of the Church.

This shows us that the practice of head covering is actually compatible with the liturgical renewal of Vatican II, where the Church respectfully studies and accepts those customs that do not offend the faith. In the spirit of *Sacrosanctum Concilium*, wherever wearing a head covering for women is seen as a "culture and tradition" of the people, it has a strong chance of being adopted once again by the Church. The revival or rediscovery of the head covering might be an expression of the genius of the faithful who preserve it even though it is not required anymore by the liturgical norm. Suppose we have the courage to evaluate and adopt something alien to the Church's practice and tradition; why don't we have enough courage to evaluate and preserve something that really comes from the bosom of the Church throughout her existence?

Canonically speaking, an abrogated code or norm under certain conditions may become a custom in the Catholic Church. Custom is defined as a long-standing practice accepted by a community. Under certain conditions, a custom can acquire the force of law according to canonical tradition. For an abrogated norm to be custom, it needs several conditions, i.e., not being expressly forbidden (cf. Canon 24),

being reasonable and conducive to the common good
(cf. Canon 24), fulfilling a prescribed time period
(cf. Canon 26), being introduced by the community
(cf. Canon 25), and being approved or tolerated by
the Church's authority (cf. Canon 23).

Now, let us examine the practice of head covering,
especially if it has been part of the local custom.

Firstly, the practice of wearing the veil for
women in the Church is not explicitly forbidden by
the universal or liturgical law of the Church. The
Church neither prohibits nor requires it. Secondly,
the reasonableness of the custom can be traced back
to biblical and patristic traditions. Thirdly, for a
practice to acquire the force of law, it must have
been observed for at least thirty continuous years
(Canon 26). If a community has followed the wearing of the head covering for women since the 1983
Code took effect, it means that they have observed
it for more than thirty years. If a community had
just rediscovered the practice in 1994, it would
have passed the requirements of "thirty continuous
years." Fourthly, the custom must be introduced by
the community. It must not be enforced by Church
authority. Lastly, the community possessing all four
requirements can request acknowledgment from
Church authority that their head covering custom
has acquired the force of law. It is the duty of the
competent authority to examine it.

So we see that there is a blessing in disguise
in this phenomenon. "In disguise," because it does
seem that we abandoned something that was handed
down to us since the time of the apostles, in order
to avoid a purported "uniformity" and "rigidity"
claimed to be incompatible with our times. "A

blessing," because this time the people would practice it through their own conscience and no longer out of a mere following of the norms.

The "revival" and the "rediscovery" of head covering for women is not something merely sentimental or nostalgic of past glory. It is a sign of how God moves the hearts of the faithful to greater reverence when approaching the altar of the Lord. It has something to do with how the Church reflects herself, examines her conduct, and prepares herself to be worthy of the heavenly banquet and to present herself as a spotless bride of the Lamb.

BIBLIOGRAPHY

CHAPTER 1

Ambrose of Milan. "*De Virginitate* (Concerning Virginity), Book III." Translated by H. de Romestin, E. de Romestin and H.T.F. Duckworth. From: *Nicene and Post-Nicene Fathers, Second Series*, Vol. 10. Ed. Philip Schaff and Henry Wace. (Buffalo, NY: Christian Literature Publishing Co., 1896.) Revised and edited for New Advent by Kevin Knight. *New Advent Catholic Encyclopedia.* 2009. www.newadvent.org/fathers/34073.htm (accessed on 14 Sep 2015)

Augustine of Hippo. "*De Virginitate* (Of Holy Virginity)." Translated by C.L. Cornish. From: *Nicene and Post-Nicene Fathers, First Series*, Vol. 3. Ed. Philip Schaff. (Buffalo, NY: Christian Literature Publishing Co., 1887.) Revised and edited for New Advent by Kevin Knight. *New Advent Catholic Encyclopedia.* 2009. www.newadvent.org/fathers/1310.htm (accessed on 14 Sep 2015)

Benedict XVI. "An Apostolic Letter Issued 'Motu Proprio,' *Summorum Pontificum*, on the Use of the Roman Liturgy Prior to the Reform of 1970." *Vatican Website.* 7 Jul 2007. http://w2.vatican.va/content/benedict-xvi/en/letters/2007/documents/hf_ben-xvi_let_20070707_lettera-vescovi.html (accessed on 15 Sep 2015)

Clement of Alexandria. "*Paedagogus* (The Instructor), Book III." Translated by William Wilson. From: *Ante-Nicene Fathers*, Vol. 2. Ed. Alexander Roberts, James Donaldson, and A. Cleveland Coxe. (Buffalo, NY: Christian Literature Publishing Co., 1885.) Revised and edited for New Advent by Kevin Knight. *New Advent Catholic Encylopedia.* 2009. www.newadvent.org/fathers/02093.htm (accessed on 14 Sep 2015)

Foederatio Internationalis *Una Voce*. "*Positio* N. 22 Headcoverings in Church in the Extraordinary Form." *FIUV Position Papers on the 1962 Missal.* December 2014. www.unavoce.ru/pdf/FIUV_PP/FIUV_PP22_Head_Covering.pdf (accessed on 14 Sep 2015)

Goodman, Donald P. "Because of the Angels: A Study of the Veil in the Christian Tradition." *Tradition in Action.* 2005. www.traditioninaction.org/religious/d005rpVeil_1_Goodman.htm (accessed on 14 Sep 2015)

John Chrysostom. "Homily 26 on First Corinthians." Translated by Talbot W. Chambers. From: *Nicene and Post-Nicene Fathers, First Series,* Vol. 12. Ed. Philip Schaff. (Buffalo, NY: Christian Literature Publishing Co., 1889.) Revised and edited for New Advent by Kevin Knight. *New Advent Catholic Encyclopedia.* 2009. www.newadvent.org/fathers/220126.htm (accessed on 14 Sep 2015)

John Paul II. "On the Dignity and Vocation of Women: Apostolic Letter, *Mulieris Dignitatem,* of the Supreme Pontiff John Paul II on the Occasion of the Marian Year." *Vatican Website.* 15 Aug 1988. http://w2.vatican.va/content/john-paul-ii/en/apost_letters/1988/documents/hf_jp-ii_apl_19880815_mulieris-dignitatem.html (accessed on 15 Sep 2015)

Konferensi Waligereja Indonesia. *Kitab Hukum Kanonik Edisi Resmi Bahasa Indonesia.* Jakarta: KWI, 2006.

Monti, James. *A Sense of the Sacred: Roman Catholic Worship in the Middle Ages.* San Francisco: Ignatius Press, 2012.

Tertullian. "*De virginibus velandis* (On the Veiling of Virgins)." Translated by S. Thelwall. From: *Ante-Nicene Fathers,* Vol. 4. Ed. Alexander Roberts, James Donaldson, and A. Cleveland Coxe. (Buffalo, NY: Christian Literature Publishing Co., 1885.) Revised and edited for New Advent by Kevin Knight. *New Advent Catholic Encyclopedia.* 2009. www.newadvent.org/fathers/0403.htm (accessed on 14 Sep 2015)

Thomas Aquinas. "*Super I Epistolam B. Pauli ad Corinthios lectura* (Commentary on the First Epistle to the Corinthians)." Translated by Fabian Larcher, O.P. *St. Thomas Aquinas' Works in English.* Dominican House of Studies, Priory of the Immaculate Conception. http://dhspriory.org/thomas/SS1Cor.htm (accessed on 15 Sep 2015)

CHAPTER 2

Catechism of the Catholic Church. Vatican City: Libreria Editrice Vaticana, 2003. www.vatican.va/archive/ENG0015/_INDEX.HTM (accessed on 29 Oct 2015)

John Paul II. "General Audience on the Intrinsic Link between the Eucharist and the Gift of the Holy Spirit." *Adoremus Bulletin.* 13 Sep 1989. www.adoremus.org/JPII-CatechesisEucharist.html#anchor411725 (accessed on 25 Oct 2015)

——. "General Audience on the Church: the Church is Revealed in Parables." *Totus2us.* 18 Sep 1989. http://totus2us.com/vocation/jpii-catechesis-on-the-church/the-church-is-revealed-in-parables/ (accessed on 25 Oct 2015)

CHAPTER 3

Augustine of Hippo. *The Confessions.* Translated by Albert C. Outler. Christian Classics Ethereal Library. www.ccel.org/a/augustine/confessions/ (accessed on 15 Sep 2015)

Benedict XVI. "On Christian Love: Encyclical Letter, *Deus Caritas Est,* of the Supreme Pontiff Benedict XVI to the Bishops, Priests, and Deacons, Men and Women Religious, and All the Lay Faithful." *Vatican Website.* December 25, 2005. http://w2.vatican.va/content/benedict-xvi/en/encyclicals/documents/hf_ben-xvi_enc_20051225_deus-caritas-est.html (accessed on 15 Sep 2015)

Devendra, Rebecca. "The Chapel Veil and a Woman's Rights." *One Peter Five.* 4 Feb 2015. www.onepeterfive.com/chapel-veil-womans-rights/ (accessed on 18 Sep 2015)

Foederatio Internationalis Una Voce. "*Positio N. 22* Headcoverings in Church in the Extraordinary Form." *FIUV Position Papers on the 1962 Missal.* December 2014. www.unavoce.ru/pdf/FIUV_PP/FIUV_PP22_Head_Covering.pdf (accessed on 14 Sep 2015)

John Paul II. *Man and Woman He Created Them: a Theology of the Body.* Boston: Pauline Books & Media, 2006. Online text of Theology of the Body may be accessed at: https://www.ewtn.com/library/PAPALDOC/JP2TBIND.HTM

Pope, Charles. "Should Women Cover Their Heads in Church?" *Archdiocese of Washington Blog.* 19 May 2010. http://blog.adw.org/2010/05/should-women-cover-their-heads-in-church/ (accessed on 18 Sep 2015)

Thomas Aquinas. *Summa Theologiae* II-II, Q. 169, art. 1. Translated by the Fathers of the English Dominican Province. *New Advent Catholic Encyclopedia.* 2008. www.newadvent.org/summa/3169.htm (accessed on 14 Sep 2015)

CHAPTER 4

Benedict XVI. "On the Eucharist as the Source and Summit of the Church's Life and Mission: Post-Synodal Apostolic Exhortation, *Sacramentum Caritatis,* of the Holy Father Benedict XVI to the Bishops, Clergy, Consecrated Persons and the Lay Faithful." *Vatican Website.* 22 Feb 2007. http://w2.vatican.va/content/benedict-xvi/en/apost_exhortations/documents/hf_ben-xvi_exh_20070222_sacramentum-caritatis.html (accessed on 16 Sep 2015)

De Sales, Francis. *An Introduction to the Devout Life.* New York: Random House, 2002.

Lewis, C.S. *Mere Christianity.* New York: Harper Collins, 2001.

Selmys, Melinda. "Before Sin: Creation, Adam and Eve, and the Garden of Eden." *This Rock Magazine* Vol. 22, No. 3, May 2011. www.catholic.com/magazine/articles/before-sin (accessed on 16 Sep 2015)

Thomas Aquinas. *Summa Theologiae* I-II, Q. 85, art. 3. Translated by the Fathers of the English Dominican Province. *New Advent Catholic Encyclopedia.* 2008. www.newadvent.org/summa/2085.htm#article3 (accessed on 15 Sep 2015)

——. "IIa-IIae, Q.169, A.1." Translated by the Fathers of the English Dominican Province. *New Advent Catholic Encyclopedia.* 2008. www.newadvent.org/summa/3169.htm (accessed on 16 Sep 2015)

CHAPTER 6

Benedict XVI. "Message for the First National Day of Young Catholics of the Netherlands." *Vatican Website.* 21 Nov 2005. https://w2.vatican.va/content/benedict-xvi/en/messages/pont-messages/2005/documents/hf_ben-xvi_mes_20051121_youth.html (accessed on 18 Oct 2015)

——. "On the Eucharist as the Source and Summit of the Church's Life and Mission: Post-Synodal Apostolic Exhortation, *Sacramentum Caritatis*, of the Holy Father Benedict XVI to the Bishops, Clergy, Consecrated Persons and the Lay Faithful." *Vatican Website.* 22 Feb 2007. http://w2.vatican.va/content/benedict-xvi/en/apost_exhortations/documents/hf_ben-xvi_exh_20070222_sacramentum-caritatis.html (accessed on 16 Sep 2015)

Congregation for Divine Worship and the Discipline of the Sacrament. "Instruction, *Redemptionis Sacramentum*, on certain matters to be observed or to be avoided regarding the Most Holy Sacrament." *Vatican Website.* Mar 2004. www.vatican.va/roman_curia/congregations/ccdds/documents/rc_con_ccdds_doc_20040423_redemptionis-sacramentum_en.html (accessed on 27 Sep 2015)

John Paul II. "On Eucharist in Its Relationship to the Church: Encyclical Letter, *Ecclesia de Eucharistia*, of His Holiness Pope John Paul II to the Bishops, Priests, and Deacons, Men and Women in the Consecrated Life, and All the Lay Faithful." *Vatican Website.* 17 Apr 2003. www.vatican.va/holy_father/special_features/encyclicals/documents/hf_jp-ii_enc_20030417_ecclesia_eucharistia_en.html (accessed on 19 Sep 2015)

Pius XII. "On the Mystical Body of Christ: Encyclical Letter, *Mystici Corporis Christi*, of Pope Pius XII to Our Venerable Brethren, Patriarchs, Primates, Archbishops, Bishops, and Other Local Ordinaries Enjoying Peace and Communion with the Apostolic See." *Vatican Website.* 29 Jun 1943. http://w2.vatican.va/content/pius-xii/en/encyclicals/documents/hf_p-xii_enc_29061943_mystici-corporis-christi.html (accessed on 19 Sep 2015)

Teresa of Avila. *Way of Perfection*. Mineola: Dover Publications, 2011.

Thomas Aquinas. *Summa Theologiae* III, Q. 80, arts. 1, 2. Translated by the Fathers of the English Dominican Province. *New Advent Catholic Encyclopedia*. 2008. www.newadvent. org/summa/4080.htm#article1 (accessed on 19 Sep 2015)

APPENDIX 1

Benedict XVI. "Homily at the Holy Mass and Eucharistic Procession to the Basilica of Saint Mary Major on the Solemnity of Corpus Christi." *Vatican Website*. 22 May 2008. http://w2.vatican.va/content/benedict-xvi/en/homilies/2008/documents/hf_ben-xvi_hom_20080522_corpus-domini.html (accessed on 8 Nov 2015)

Council of Trent (1545-1563). "The Sacraments: The Holy Eucharist—Necessity of Previous Preparation for Communion." *Catechism of the Council of Trent*. www.catholicapologetics.info/thechurch/catechism/Holy7Sacraments-Eucharist.shtml (accessed on 8 Nov 2015)

Filipazzi, Antonio Guido. "Homily at the Opening Mass of the Third Asian Apostolic Congress on Mercy." Medan, 14 Oct 2015.

Ratzinger, Joseph Cardinal. "Address to Catechists and Religion Teachers 'On the New Evangelization,' on the Jubilee of Catechists and Religion Teachers." *EWTN*. December 10, 2000. https://www.ewtn.com/new_evangelization/Ratzinger.htm (accessed on 8 Nov 2015)

——. *God Is Near Us*. San Francisco: Ignatius Press, 2003.

——. *The Spirit of the Liturgy*. San Francisco: Ignatius Press, 2000.

Thomas Aquinas. "Oratio Altera Post Communionem." Translated and edited by Robert Anderson and Johann Moser. *The Aquinas Prayer Book*. Manchester: Sophia Institute Press, 2000.

——. "Oratio Ante Communionem." Translated and edited by Robert Anderson and Johann Moser. *The Aquinas Prayer Book*. Manchester: Sophia Institute Press, 2000.

ACKNOWLEDGMENTS

ALL PRAISES AND GLORY TO OUR LORD Jesus Christ, truly present in the Blessed Sacrament, Spouse of my soul and Provision for my earthly pilgrimage. I can only reciprocate His most beautiful crown of thorns with my unworthy little mantilla.

Endless gratitude to my heavenly family, invisible yet very much present and alive: the Blessed Mother, Saint Joseph, Saint Dominic, Saint Thomas Aquinas, Saint Catherine of Siena, Saint Teresa of Avila, and the Holy Angels.

My deep thanks to His Excellency Antonio Guido Filipazzi, the Apostolic Nuncio to Indonesia when this book was first published, for his willingness to read and correct the very first draft, and to provide his Foreword. His love for the Sacraments inspired me.

To the publishing team at Dioma: thank you for giving this book its first opportunity to see the light of day.

To friends and acquaintances who contributed their testimonials: know that your voices reached, and continue to reach, thousands of souls!

To Dr. Peter Kwasniewski and Os Justi Press — thank you for graciously letting this little book have its second birth. In your hands, and according to His mighty providence, may it bring many more souls to the life of virtue.

To the people most dear to my heart: Abram, Filomena, Father Bayu Ruseno, OP, Robertus Silveriano, OP, and my mother and father. "Every time I think of you I thank God for you. I have joy in my heart every time I ask God to help you. I thank God for the joy we share in telling the good news from the very first day until now" (Phil 1:3–5).

ABOUT THE AUTHOR

ANNA ELISSA, OP, is a wife, mother, psychiatrist, and Lay Dominican from Bogor, Indonesia. She earned her medical degree from Universitas Pelita Harapan and completed her psychiatry residency at Universitas Indonesia. Her spiritual interests include, but are not limited to, Thomistic theology on the soul, the interplay between faith and mental health, Church art and traditions, and Eucharistic devotions.